"What a journey Dan has taken. He was forty-eight when we started working together in Central Washington farm country. After living his whole life in big cities, he was suddenly living at the base of the Cascade Mountains with great hiking and skiing less than an hour away. Since his family didn't join him until the end of the school year, Dan started exploring the area on the weekends. On Mondays, he shared his weekend adventures, often things I hadn't experienced after living here for decades. Within a couple of years, Dan had climbed Mount Rainier, we were frequently downhill skiing together, and he was fast making friends with other outdoor sportsmen. He embraced the increasingly technical activities of backcountry skiing and serious mountaineering, and before my eyes completed the transformation from city slicker to outdoor adventurer."

— Tom Hurson, President, CEO, Tree Top Inc. (ret.)

"I have had the joy of spending many a day wandering the hills and mountains with Dan. His optimistic approach to life made hard days easier on those who went on these adventures. It also helped save him on his wildest adventure of all—trapped under the ice on the Grand Teton."

— Pete Shepard, Vice President of Supply Chain, Reeser's Fine Foods

"When Dan told me the story of the 'Fall,' we both broke down in tears together. His close friendship through the years culminated in that candid conversation of the survival of the fall and all the events that could have lent to his death. We shared in the spirituality of how some force (God) had a hand in his being alive today. Dan always was adventuresome and yearned for the extreme. In this book, he shares this extreme experience and how it shook the core of his being so that he cherishes life even more every day. After all this, he asks, 'How am I doing?' I have the deepest admiration for him and the friendship we share."

— Alex Reethof, Founder and CEO, Gathering Industries, Inc. 501(c)(3)

"Appreciating life and what it has to offer often comes to us only after we have been faced with losing it…in one split second. Dan is a lifelong friend, and after his accident, I noticed a change in his values, his appreciation of moments and family, and a closer understanding of *why*."

— John O'Hara, Vice President of Business Development, TVS Design

"When Dan invites you on an adventure, just say, 'Yes' and know you are part of a select and fortunate group. He will lead or let you lead, but mostly, he is just there at your side. Prepare to train and suffer, but also to laugh as you journey into the beauty that can only be experienced in the wilderness. A day on the trail with Dan is guaranteed to leave you tired but also happy. He will push you to prepare, knowing it is not only for your safety but ultimate enjoyment. There is no one better to spend a day or weeks with on the trail or in life. The places we've traveled together are challenging and rigorous hiking destinations, but also spectacular and at the top of a list of lifetime memories."

— Reg Blackburn, Managing Director, The Braff Group (ret.)

"When I think of people I wish were my best friend, Dan Wenker is at the top of the list. He's unassuming and darkly funny. Thank God he lived through his fall in the Tetons so I could profit from his story on every backpacking trip I lead. I tell his story around the campfire like it's folklore, and by association, I earn trail cred. I've told family and friends of my badass friend Dan. I've inspired other retirees to keep adventuring through Dan tales, and I've scared others into safety precautions. He's a hero of mine and of most people I take hiking."

— Sara Mack, Senior Program Leader and Coordinator for No Barriers; REI Outdoor Experiences Guide

"Working with and learning from Dan while at REI was such a pleasure. He's incredibly knowledgeable and kind (with a killer sense of humor), and I am truly thankful we have maintained this friendship with our 'circle of trust' (including Sarah, of course). Not only is Dan brilliant, but as this harrowing tale goes to show, he's resilient. His story is an inspiring reminder that you may be down, but you are never out. It's also a sobering but valuable story for anyone who spends time outdoors: 'The wilderness isn't personal.'"

— Juli Yoder, REI Outdoor Experiences Guide

"I've known Dan for more than twenty years. We have helped each other out by listening to work challenges, worked through raising our kids together, and experienced all of life's many turns and obstacles. Dan is a strong man in faith, in conscience, in honor, and above all in loyalty. Dan's life journey found him retired too young, and he was struggling to decide where his next chapter was going to take him. He has always been an outdoorsman—hiking, skiing, mountain climbing. But Dan was still looking for more. Then came the 'Experience' in the Tetons; the transformation was amazing! Read his story and take the opportunity to win back the positive in your life. What a story!"

— Dee Duncan, President, CEO Keyston Bros.

"I'm privileged to have had Dan as a friend for forty years. His disciplined approach to life and fitness most likely saved his life as told in this harrowing tale. Treat yourself to a great read."

— Doug Corbett, Director of Sales and Marketing,
JW Marriott Marco Island

"Having the unique blend of resilience and lightheartedness in life not only eases tension but also highlights the power of laughter in overcoming adversity. During our time working together in the outdoor adventure field, Dan and I frequently discussed the mindset required to navigate everything from daily struggles to life-altering events. His insight and magnetic character help him thrive even in the toughest circumstances, especially when at the bottom of a hole."

— Hope Oldham, Supervisor of Field Experiences, REI Co-Op

"Just when you think you know a guy, he goes off to scale the Grand Teton and slides into an ice moat, breaks his leg, and survives. Then he writes a book about it. Amazing. When Dan told me he had taken up mountaineering, my first reaction was, "What—why?" After reading his book, I now know why. I'm also convinced that Dan has an in with God, sort of a Divine Insurance

Policy, and armed with that coverage, he has decided he might as well make the most of the time he has on this earth while he can, which he does. We should all have half the excitement Dan creates in his life and then brings back to us in *Staying on Guard*."

— Mike Parham, Managing Partner, Catalysta, Partners, LLC

"*Staying on Guard* is a riveting exploration of self-discovery and resilience in the great outdoors. Dan's journey from city life to mountaineering mastery inspires readers to embrace nature's challenges, prioritize physical fitness, and live life to the fullest. A must-read for anyone looking for adventure and personal transformation."

— Susan Friedmann, CSP, International Bestselling Author of *Riches in Niches: How to Make It BIG in a small Market*

"*Staying on Guard* is a true story of overcoming odds and not letting fear hold you back from enjoying life. Dan Wenker has something to teach us all—you're never too old to climb a mountain or pursue whatever goal you have your heart set upon in creating your own destiny. Whether you're a risk-taker, adventurer, or just want to be more physically active, this book will inspire you to do more and be more."

— Patrick Snow, Publishing Coach and International Bestselling Author of *Creating Your Own Destiny* and *The Affluent Entrepreneur*

"Dan Wenker shares the truths about mountain climbing and any other risky activities, including that while fear is healthy, it need not hold us back, just help us make better decisions, and that few things compare to summiting a mountain, so why not go out and have an adventure? I thoroughly enjoyed this book, marveled at the synchronicities in it, and have no doubt Dan's story will inspire countless readers."

— Nicole Gabriel, Author of *Finding Your Inner Truth* and *Stepping Into Your Becoming*

"I greatly admire Dan Wenker, a man who when most start thinking of retiring and taking it easy, decided it was time to start climbing mountains. He's now climbed numerous mountains on two continents, and I suspect he isn't done yet. Even his harrowing accident that he details in this book did not stop him. Let him reaffirm for you that life is full of possibilities when we are open to them."

— Tyler R. Tichelaar, PhD and Award-Winning Author of *Odin's Eye: A Marquette Time Travel Novel*

A MOUNTAINEER'S MEMOIR OF SURVIVING NEAR–DEATH
AFTER FALLING INTO AN ICE MOAT

STAYING
ON GUARD

A SPIRITUAL ENCOUNTER OF MIRACLES AND GRATITUDE
TO DISCOVER LIFE'S PURPOSE

DAN WENKER

AVIVA
PUBLISHING
New York

DEDICATION

To my wife, Mary: Your dedication to me and our family over the years is testimony to the phrase "unconditional love." This book would not have happened without your guidance and support. Our home would not be the nurturing, warm place it is without you.

To our children, Daniel and Caroline: The miracles who came into our life and make us proud. You are two of the most phenomenal people I know. Life became complete when you were born.

To my parents, Muriel and Allen Wenker: You built a home on a solid foundation of love and faith from day one, and you pushed your children to be independent people who should take risks.

To my good friend Pete Matheson (1961-2017), who tragically died too early during a hiking accident. His memory and the times we shared with our wives are eternally saved in my heart; they fill the void created by not having him on earth. His booming voice whispers to me often.

To both the weekend adventurer and the pro mountaineers: People who push themselves—sometimes to the extreme—just to get the most out of life by experiencing the awe of the wilderness.

To all mountain search and rescue personnel worldwide.

ACKNOWLEDGMENTS

I would like to thank the following for their roles in my life and the creation of this book:

The Jenny Lake Park Rangers—the unsung heroes of the wilderness.

The many friends who heard about my accident and touched me with their kind words from the heart, and who suggested I write it all down to share. Meg McLeroy, thank you for your sympathetic, understanding ear and wise counsel. Thank you to my cousin Dean Borig and Christine Miles for introducing me to Patrick Snow, who unlocked the therapeutic mystery of book writing.

Nancy Robbins for helping to provide a soft landing when we moved to Yakima.

Pete Shepard for exposing me to the world of mountaineering and his patience during our initial training sessions.

Foursquare Mountaineering—especially Doug White, Mark McGuire, David Stoothoff, Dennis Elliott, Ron Cowan, and Jim Zingerman—for preventing me from becoming a "one-and-done" climber.

Tom Hurson and Greg Bainter for agreeing to interview me and offer me a job at Tree Top, Inc. in Yakima, Washington, which dramatically changed my life's path.

Dr. John Baranowski, Lisa Baldoz, Ned and Kathryn Rawn, and Two Mountains Winery—we will always consider Yakima home because of your friendship.

Scott Summers, for welcoming me to Yakima and opening your house to me while my family was in transit.

Corey Buhay and Louisa Albanese with *Backpacker Magazine*, and Luke Thompson with the *Yakima-Herald Republic* for documenting our accident.

REI Co-Op Outdoor Experiences Team—Atlanta—Sarah & Juli (circle of trust), Hope, Garrett, Clay, Sylvia, Ashley, and Julani.

My book production team, my editor, Tyler Tichelaar, and my book designer, Nicole Gabriel.

SPECIAL ACKNOWLEDGMENT

While it's hard to put into words how to properly acknowledge Jim Zingerman for saving my life, I find it best to use the divinely inspired Bible verse found in John 15:13: "Greater love has no one than this: to lay down one's life for one's friends." Thanks, Jim, for not giving up. Thanks for your plea in the wilderness, and thanks for digging into the side of that hill and disregarding the danger you put your own life in by holding onto that rope when all seemed lost.

Jim and I were good friends before the potentially fatal accident in June 2022. After the accident, our friendship dramatically increased to a level few people can understand. As I stated in my thank you note to him just after we returned home, "I truly believe that you were touched by God that day." My note also included, "Like it or not, the tears shed that day and the experience have bound us together forever."

Many people casually say they *"have your back"* when the conversation comes up about how close a friend they are. With Jim, there is no question. I know he would risk his life in order to save mine. For that, I am eternally grateful.

STAYING
ON GUARD

Dan Wenker

CONTENTS

FOREWORD

ALONE ON THE HIGH MOUNTAIN

by
Jim Zingerman, MD

I just watched my friend Dan sail by and disappear over the cliff into the icy waters below. *What now?* I thought. *How life will be forever changed.* Then I heard him call my name! *He's alive! How can I possibly help him? He may freeze. He may be injured. He may...* What comes next is our life-changing story.

Dan Wenker and I developed a close friendship through the sport of mountaineering. We were introduced by mutual friends with the same passion. As we approached challenging peaks, Dan would reflect back the nervous grin I was also feeling. We forged a bond through shared adventure. We learned to trust one another, knowing that to the best of our ability, we each had the other's back. This unspoken promise was to be tested in a way neither of us ever could have imagined.

Success when venturing a mountain climb requires hours of pre-planning with efforts toward route finding for the best approach and gear finding to lighten the load. We understood the risks and worked to reduce the chance of getting in harm's way. Hiking the Grand Teton was quite different from the "Let's have fun" approach of my youth, climbing "hills" in the Northeast. We needed to partner with someone who could teach us the ways of the mountain as well as join together with those who could help each other in times of trouble.

When I began thinking about climbing mountains in the northwestern United States, my focus was taking on a challenge that presented itself right outside my window each morning. Snowcapped peaks appeared to call to me as a playground of fun for weekends off of work. Strapping on my backpack, I set out to give it a try. Quickly into the hiking experience, I realized something was very different about these mountains.

At the trailhead, I began to ask why other hikers had gear I was unfamiliar with, such as ice axes, crampons, shovels, and a two-foot-long metal piece whose purpose I could not make out. Some had bundles of sticks with bright-colored ribbons attached. They definitely had better boots and ski poles for walking. Cell phones were just becoming common when I started, and they didn't have much coverage or carry enough charge. What I discovered was that people were much better prepared than I was for taking on these snow-capped mountains. They had grit and a look of determination on their faces.

In this powerful book by Dan Wenker, you will learn what it means to develop the skills and mental attitude needed to climb mountains. You will also gain the rich reward of sharing these experiences with acquaintances who will become lifelong friends through the bond of shared adventure.

In *Staying on Guard*, you will acquire the specific knowledge and skills needed to achieve a successful climb. Skills take time spent at home packing and repacking, going to the park in your hometown to practice each gear piece and maneuver, and asking such questions as "What if this happens?" or "What if an item is not functioning correctly?"

Through Dan's stories, you will realize you have the drive to follow your dream to a stunning summit and develop your own sense of summit fever. Let Dan Wenker be your guide to laying the groundwork you will need to navigate successfully in a sport that you can enjoy over and over again.

Jim Zingerman, MD

PREFACE: A NOTE TO THE READER

Please make certain to consult with your physician before attempting any strenuous activity. When hiking and climbing in the outdoors, be sure to have the correct equipment and be in good physical condition. Avoid hiking alone; always hike with a partner who is familiar with the mountain.

Always make certain you carry a cell phone with you and leave your hiking plan with a loved one so they know where you are.

Always pack enough food and water in case of an emergency. Remember to carry the ten essentials: map, compass, sunglasses/sunscreen, extra clothing, headlamp/flashlight, first aid supplies, fire starter, matches, knife, and extra food.

Never climb a mountain you are not properly trained to climb. That includes those that may require ropes, carabiners, and harnesses.

INTRODUCTION

"WHAT IFS" VERSUS "NOT ANYMORES"

"I have learned that clearing your mind to find your way through life comes to people in many ways and in many places. Mine has for most of my life always been in the mountains. I consider myself lucky to have at different times found the very edge of me—always somewhere right in the middle of suffering, beauty, anguish, and accomplishment! That is why I climb!"

— Mark McGuire, Mountaineer

I am purposely opening this book with a powerful quote my good friend Mark McGuire wrote a few years ago. It summarizes the impact the outdoors and mountains can have on your life. The mountains will entice you; they will pull you in; they will embrace you; they will expose your weaknesses; they will punish you if you're careless; they will push you to the edge; and they will give you a sense of elation that few activities can.

By one estimate, more than 100,000 rescues take place in the United States wilderness every year. Approximately 243 people die annually on National Park Service lands. With nearly 312 million visits annually, it works out to a death rate of less than one in a million. Heart disease, drownings, and falls are the most common reasons for fatalities. In 2024, the odds of dying in a car crash are around one in ninety-three—making it the leading cause of death in the United States, higher than the chance of dying in a fall while climbing a mountain.

While I never thought much about the subject matter of death before June 30, 2022, the real possibility presented itself when I least expected. Death is inevitable, but it's realization can make life more abundant, exciting, and vibrant! What are you doing to make your life full and exciting? What decisions are you making today to give yourself the best chance to live a long and healthy life? How are you making your life better? When you're outside or in the wilderness, what are you doing to make certain you are correctly weighing the risks so that catastrophes are prevented?

I've been in your shoes. I know what it's like to reach middle age and ask, "Which path do I want to take going forward—a path of low activity where I gradually lose the ability to do some of the things I currently love doing, or one where I take an active role so I'm positioned to have options and do exciting things in the prime of my life?" The important thing is to always stay on guard, be aware of the path you're on, and determine if it's the path you prefer.

If you're already putting yourself out there doing exciting things, that's awesome! However, I've also been there, so caught up in the moment of enjoying beautiful surroundings while doing something a little risky that I forget to weigh the risk and apply the safety measures I was taught. Next thing I know, I'm in a desperate position—risking severe injury or possible death—because I wasn't *staying on guard*.

Being exposed to the mountains and mountaineering has had a dramatic impact on my life. It has positively changed me in ways tough to explain. I'm writing this book for two reasons. The first is to demonstrate you can remain active in your mid to later years so that you continue to enjoy great outdoor activities. Staying active can be accomplished by setting a tangible goal and having a small amount of discipline. The benefits are a more abundant life that starts to take on a life of its own. You feel better because you're staying active, which allows you to do things you never thought possible. Next thing you know, you're starting to challenge yourself with the "what ifs" versus "not anymores."

I'm also writing this book for those who enjoy the outdoors and love spending time in the wilderness doing exciting things. Always be on guard! It doesn't matter if you're tackling a challenging mountain, taking on a more extreme ski slope, or just hiking in the woods. Mother Nature is impersonal. She plays no favorites and does not discriminate over who gets punished and who gets rewarded. Bad things can happen in an instant. As you're out in the world or in the wilderness, it's up to you to stay on guard so you minimize the risk.

I'm a guy who grew up in the city but happened to move to an area that promoted an outdoor lifestyle. After moving to the Pacific Northwest, I experienced how expansive the outdoors is and wondered, *What if?* I was fortunate to get involved with guys who loved the outdoors and enjoyed pushing themselves physically. As a result, I've experienced how getting into good physical condition at a later stage in life can open doors you never could have imagined. I've seen things I never thought existed or that I had only seen in books or on a *National Geographic* special. Since that time, I've been able to climb some of the tallest peaks in the US and the tallest in Africa.

Those adventures never would have happened if I hadn't taken that one small step, decided to improve my physical condition, and then gradually stepped up my goals. While doing these activities, I've also let my guard down, resulting in a near-death experience that would challenge the deepest part of me. Falling into an ice moat, deep below the snow's surface, brought to light how quickly things can happen in the wilderness. The accident occurred not because of the dangers inherent in the wilderness, but because I didn't stay on guard and use the basic measures taught in every beginner mountaineering class.

Life is busy. Life is challenging. Getting into decent physical condition is tough…at the start. You may start every year with a New Year's resolution to get in better shape, only to have life happen so that the forward momentum stops a month into your plan. While reading this book, consider some of the things you did to stay on the conditioning path. Once you've seen the other side of getting into decent physical condition, the time invested may just keep you on course so that you avoid stopping and going back to where you were. Keeping up a regimen prevents you from experiencing the painful startup again. I firmly believe anyone can get there.

Accidents in the outdoors happen. No need to experience a lot of angst about what can happen so you're paranoid while walking down the trail. We're all human. Once you get involved in the outdoors, you want to take it all in and get in a meditative state so that you have the mental release you're looking for. The thought is just to be aware, be smart, weigh the risks, and be prepared if something bad does happen.

So, come on; take the small step to start getting in better shape. People in their sixties and seventies are setting records for climbing, skiing, endurance racing, and much more. Learn about them and how they got to that point. You may find they were just like you, got a late start, and then rocked the world with their accomplishments! Also, be aware and prepared when you're in the wilderness. Have the right equipment and use it when the appropriate situation arises. Take those couple of minutes to be aware and see danger before it negatively impacts you. Take a course to learn preventative measures so you're prepared. It could just save your life.

Although I began writing this book to tell the story of my mountaineering, my outdoor journey, and my near-death experience, it also reinforces my desire to get more people active so they can enjoy life the way I've been able to. I hope it influences you in a positive way to get in better condition and experience the wonder and beauty of the outdoors, if you're not doing so already. If you already are, please stay on guard while you're enjoying the wilderness and all it has to offer. If I can get one person to do that, all this writing therapy will be well worth it.

So, I challenge you to find your reason to climb toward achieving your goals, practicing gratitude daily, and discovering your life's purpose!

Dan Wenker

StayingOnGuard.org

CHAPTER 1

REFUSING TO GIVE UP

"Only those who will risk going too far can
possibly find out how far one can go."

— T. S. Eliot

Have you ever found yourself staring death right in the face? Maybe it happened during a car crash, or near drowning, or some life-changing event when you saw your entire life flash in front of your eyes? Did you panic or remain calm? How did you successfully navigate your way back to safety?

Ultimately, I came face-to-face with death on June 30, 2022, at the age of sixty-two. When I came to my senses, I realized that while climbing down from the Lower Saddle on the Grand Teton in the Teton Range in Wyoming, at about 10,000 feet, I had fallen sixty feet into a frigid ice moat under the ice after sliding into a gap in the snow. An ice moat is a crevasse in the snow or ice; it is formed by an underground stream or waterfall and drops an unknown depth into the earth. Inside that ice moat, I experienced pure darkness. When I looked up, I saw a tiny opening of sunlight twelve to twenty-four inches wide.

I was not sure how I had dropped through a tiny opening—I felt like a golf ball when it goes in for a hole in one. What were the odds? A raging waterfall was to my right that continued down into a pitch-black abyss. A solid ice wall was behind me, another ice wall was to my left, and a solid rock wall was in front of me that was slick from water spraying on it without any chance of climbing. At that point, I realized I was standing on a narrow ice platform that was three-feet wide and ten-feet long.

My hands were scratched up and so cold I repeatedly put them in my mouth to warm them, one at a time. I knew I would need them if there was any hope of getting out. How would I ever escape from this loud, cold, watery perch? It felt like I was sixty feet below the ground in a dark dungeon. Then I heard a subconscious voice clearly speak. "Remain calm. Breathe slowly." I knew the calmer I could remain, the clearer I would be able to think. Panic did not seem to be an option. It would only lead to a negative spiral. I needed to keep my thoughts clear. Soon after, I heard a prophetic voice. *"Today is not your day to die."* While the voice was somewhat calming, I found it almost impossible to believe I could get out of there alive.

I started looking for a way to climb up the slippery rock face in front of me. I felt the sheer rock wall in front of me and couldn't find a rock to hold; they were too small or not solid enough to hold my weight. The wall was straight up vertically with a thin sheet of moisture that made it slick. There didn't seem like a way out. After about twenty-five minutes on the thin ledge, I shouted to my climbing partner, Jim Zingerman. In a long, drawn-out cadence, I was calling "Jiiiimmmm! Jiiiiimmmm!" in an uncontrolled manner. It was strange to call out his name. When I was alone in my thoughts and not calling out, I was calm. When I started calling Jim's name, I heard a sense of panic in my voice and became more emotional. The more I called out, the more emotional I seemed to become; it was a desperate plea simply to hear a voice answer, though I knew the loud waterfall would muffle any sounds coming down.

I looked down at my feet and noticed the Seattle Kraken hat I had been wearing. My son had given it to me for my birthday the year before. I thought about grabbing it, feeling bad that I might lose a gift he had given me. Just before reaching for it, I pulled back, concerned that if I moved too much on the ledge, it would give way and I would fall into the cold darkness below me. I also started thinking about the conversation I'd had with my wife Mary when we had separated at the Salt Lake City airport a few days before. My daughter had just gotten married a couple of days before. I told Mary this climb would be the most technical one I had attempted. "If something happens to me, don't call Caroline on her honeymoon and ruin the event."

The Yakima climbing group I had been involved with had done some crevasse climbing one afternoon at the Nisqually Glacier on Mount Rainier. We would repel down, then climb up the ice wall using ice axes with crampons on our feet to slowly scale the ice wall. Although this surrounding was familiar, this situation was dire since all I had were my hands and legs to climb out. No ropes, no axes, no crampons…nothing! Thinking I might be experiencing my last minutes on earth, I then felt a slight tap on my right shoulder. The ledge was completely dark. When I turned my head, I couldn't see anything.

Reaching my left arm around, I realized a climbing rope was tapping my shoulder. A rope! A rope! I didn't stop to think about where it was coming from. Instead, I grabbed the rope, tugged on it three times, and then pulled it down far enough to have enough slack to wrap it around my waist and tie it in a knot. Rescuers must be at the top to pull me up. No pull came, so I wrapped the rope around my right hand, then my left, to have a couple of safety valves in case the rope came untied around my waist.

Once I had the rope secured, I leaned back and started what can best be described as a reverse rappel up the sheer rock wall. It was a slow, agonizing walk and pull up a flat rock face. Step-by-step, I would breathe slowly, take two pulls, and then walk up the wall with my body perpendicular to the rock face. About halfway up the wall, behind and in front of me, the opening started to narrow. I leaned back farther and was able to wedge my back against the wall behind me while pressing forward with my legs in front of me to relieve the rope's pressure. I would feel the slack being pulled in as I ascended the wall slowly, one foot at a time, making my way to the small opening that the sun was shining through. This process of climbing up the wall lasted about twenty to thirty minutes.

"In every walk with nature, one receives far more than he seeks."

— John Muir

Once I reached the opening and stuck my head out, I could see Jim alone, sitting crouched another fifteen feet above me with his end of the rope wrapped around him. When I saw that huge Latvian smile of Jim's, relief flooded over me. I might just survive the fall after all. His first words will forever ring in my ears. "Dan, it's so good to see your face!" I rested on a small ledge, then continued pulling myself up the wall until I was just below Jim's feet.

"Where should I go?" I asked in desperation.

"Jump on top of me," Jim said.

I did that and Jim placed his coat on top of me. I was shivering uncontrollably from being in that cold, wet hole. The combination of Jim's coat and the heat generated by the sun on the rocks was euphoric! We both lay there on the rocks in a full embrace, laughing and crying, realizing it was a miraculous moment!

After the moment of elation passed, we became aware that our trial was not over. Although I had made it out of the ice moat, we were on a steep, forty-five-to-fifty-degree sloped solid rock incline way above the tree line in the wilderness at about 10,600 feet of elevation. Because we decided to glissade, we were now approximately 200 feet below the trail in a canyon without a way to get out, except for scaling another rock wall straight up. By this time, my left hip and back were starting to throb. My left leg had a dull pain, but it seemed workable. I lay perfectly still, afraid to move from fear of sliding back into the ice moat I had just climbed out of. I worried I had injured myself more than I realized because of how frigidly cold I was, with the potential onset of shock based on my outdoor first aid courses. Jim informed me at that time that he did not have cell phone coverage and could not communicate outside the canyon.

The day was rapidly ending. We both knew in a few hours it would be evening. Because it was so early in the year, we knew the temperatures would drop quickly once the sun went down. Jim secured me with the rope to a rock higher up. I couldn't see where he had tied me off, but I could hear him frantically blowing his rescue whistle in hopes someone hiking by would hear it. Hikers and climbers are not as frequent on the trail early in the season as they are in July and August. How were we supposed to get out and down to the trailhead?

WHAT I LEARNED

The worst thing you can do in a life-or-death situation is panic. Panic is your enemy. Panic will cloud your thoughts. Panic will cost you your life. Remaining calm is what led to being in a good state of mind when that rope tapped me on the shoulder. I also feel that the voices were God speaking to me at the time and stating it *wasn't* my time. Every day is a gift for me after that afternoon on June 30, 2022, when things could easily have gone the wrong way, ending in my death.

I also learned the importance of training for the unexpected when getting ready for a climb. My regular exercise training routine includes some upper body strengthening I knew I would need in a minor way while ascending The Grand. Little did I know that the extra strength would be vital to me when climbing out on my own since it would have been impossible for Jim to pull me out by himself. Exercise, any exercise—even if you're not climbing mountains—is better than becoming sedentary. Any extra strength will always be beneficial—even if you're not stuck at the bottom of an ice moat.

FIVE THOUGHTS TO HELP YOU REFUSE TO GIVE UP

1. Always listen to your inner voice, gut feeling, or intuition.
2. Focus on breathing and staying calm, regardless of the danger at hand.
3. Prioritize your body's safety so you have the strength to respond.
4. Carefully and calmly plan your escape or rescue.
5. Always hike with a partner when you're deep in the wilderness.

SUMMARY

"It's not the mountain we conquer, but ourselves."

— Sir Edmund Hillary

Sometimes, life happens to us, and we get in over our heads, as I did by being sixty feet under the ground, staring death in the face. I had to conquer the mountain and conquer my mind. Because I imagined I wouldn't be able to get out on my own, I needed to do things to prepare me to get out. When you are staring death in the face, I encourage you to stay calm, avoid panic, and think clearly. Once you can put your mindset in survival mode and come up with a plan for escape and survival, you must refuse to give up and believe you will live through this catastrophe. Because at the end of the day, your level of belief in you may be the only thing that keeps you alive.

So, I challenge you, when doing crazy, off-the-grid adventures, to always have a partner with you. I challenge you to always bring and use the correct gear. I challenge you to train year-round so your body is strong enough to conquer any mountain or adversity you face. And finally, I challenge you, despite having all odds stacked against you as I did sixty feet underground at 10,000 vertical feet in the mountains, to never give up. I challenge you to eternally refuse to give up!

CHAPTER 2

REMEMBERING YOUR FAMILY

"Keep your mind fixed on what you want in life:
not on what you don't want."

— Napoleon Hill

Your family and upbringing determine your destiny in many ways. That's my belief. I'm blessed to have had a good home life growing up. I was born on November 19, 1959, and I lived all of my early years through high school in Northeast Philadelphia. We lived in a stand-alone home compared to many of my high school friends who lived in attached homes—either row or twins. My dad was an inspector for the City of Philadelphia school system; my mom was a part-time nurse at a family practice doctor's office. My parents worked hard but never showed it.

My siblings and I all pitched in doing chores in the evenings while my mom worked. Because my dad worked for the public school system, he was off when we were off. As a result, spring break at the Wenkers' consisted of a multi-day work project around the house. There was no asking, bribing, or enticing; we just did it. I look back on those project weeks as character builders (in a good way).

My parents did a phenomenal job of managing a tight budget. I thought we were privileged—we were blessed, but not well off. Our three-bedroom, 1.5-baths house stretched almost 1,200 square feet. My parents were in the bedroom at the top of the stairs to the right; my brother Dave and I shared a room to the left; and my sister Barb was in the room at the end of the short hall just past the full bathroom. We all went to public school, including Barb, who attended the Pennsylvania School for the Deaf.

We lived just within the city limits because it was a requirement of the Philadelphia School District where my dad worked. My mom worked three houses down so she could be home during the day, and she didn't have to work weekends. Even though we lived within the city limits, our neighborhood had numerous trees. We played hockey and stickball (in the street), and we generally lived a life balanced between a quasi-suburb and the city. We had much better surroundings than in the city where the trees were scarce.

My parents kept us active via sports and music. They supported us taking chances, even though they were extremely risk-averse. They wanted us to grow up to be independent and to have experiences they didn't get the chance to. Barb, who was four years older than me, was a great athlete in high school. Being deaf never held her back from doing what she wanted. Although many looked at her as different, her deafness never differentiated her; it was just part of who she was. I always loved her spirit and willingness to put herself out there. Dave, who was five years older than me, was the most sensible of the three of us; he always strove to do the right thing. I looked up to and respected him enormously. As the youngest sibling, I was able to push my independence to new levels within our family.

By the time I reached high school, my brother and sister were pretty much on their own. My parents continued to support my risk-taking because I was the youngest. They were significantly less strict with me than they had been with Dave. Risk was a good thing; taking chances was rewarded as long as I stayed under the radar and didn't force them into a situation where I needed to be disciplined. I graduated from high school with average grades, then went off to college at Penn State, first at a branch campus outside of Philadelphia, and then to the main campus in central Pennsylvania.

After college, I moved to Hilton Head Island, South Carolina, to start the next stage of my life adventure hundreds of miles from home. I was the first of our family to move so far away. My parents thought I was taking a chance, but they supported my decision since the economy was in a severe slump in 1981 and jobs were hard to find in the Philadelphia area. I thought my move was a natural next step in my adventure. Slightly more than a year later, I moved to Atlanta, Georgia, where I eventually met my wife, Mary. Her blue eyes and blonde hair mesmerized me from the start. She was independent, spirited, professional, and smart, and she had a calming demeanor. She was the first woman I trusted enough to spend my life with.

We were married in 1987. A few years later, Mary and I decided to start a family. Caroline was born in July 1991. Bringing her home to raise was one of the scariest days of our lives. We were so afraid she would break that we slept on the floor by the bassinet the first night. Daniel was born eighteen months after Caroline in January 1993. By the time we brought him home, we felt confident he would be safe with us. We had the perfect little family. Then, in 1995, we made our first move to Pittsburgh, Pennsylvania, because I had received a promotion with Heinz.

Moving is exciting. It offers changes and the chance to experience new things. Pittsburgh, although a good city with lots of opportunity, was not a good move for our family. In 1997, I found a job that moved us back to Atlanta. We stayed there until 2007 while our children grew up in the suburbs. With manicured lawns, country clubs, and friends who all had respected professional occupations, we thought we were in the perfect place to raise a family for the rest of our lives. However, after a couple of job hiccups, I found myself looking for employment and came across an exciting opportunity in Yakima, Washington. "Where exactly is that?" Mary asked. "I'm not sure," I replied, "but I plan to look on the map before I go to the interview on Monday." Our children were thirteen and fifteen at the time.

Yakima is located about 145 miles, two-and-a-half hours southeast, and worlds away from Seattle in the rural, high desert area of Washington State where the majority of the country's apples and pears are grown. Many consider it God's country—moving there was a dramatic change in surroundings for our family—especially for a guy who grew up in the city, a woman who spent her entire life in big city suburbs, and two children who had lived in a planned golf/tennis neighborhood most of their lives. Caroline later summed up our move when she wrote in her college essay, "When I got off the plane in Yakima, we started driving. By the time we got to our house, I swore there was more livestock in the area than people." It was a big change.

> *"Climb the mountains and get their good tidings. Nature's peace will flow into you as sunshine flows into the trees."*
>
> *— John Muir*

Caroline looked at the move as an adventure since she would be going away to college in a couple of years. Daniel, although it took him longer to adjust, soon embraced the Northwest. They both came to love the Northwest and the outdoor lifestyle it promoted. Hiking, skiing, snowboarding, mountain biking, acres of orchards, fast-moving streams, and beautiful national parks were either located within walking distance or a short drive away. And the mountains! Everywhere you looked, tremendous mountains rose to heights hard to believe. Plus, completely natural expanses of land existed that I had never thought existed—especially for a guy who grew up in the city. From our home in the West Valley area, we could see the perpetually snowcapped peak of Mount Adams at 12,276 feet as if it were a short walk away.

Taking a chance and uprooting your family for a job (or just to move) can devastate a family. I'm fortunate to have two adventurous children and a wife who is willing to give change a try. Moving to Yakima was one of the best things that happened to our family. However, many people, when they move, will repeatedly state, "I used to be able to do this or that in such and such city before I moved." Huge mistake! You must be willing to give a new area a try, jump in, meet the people, and embrace the culture. If the people aren't friendly, find people who are also new to the area and trying to take it on.

Yakima changed all our lives in so many ways. If we hadn't given it a try and instead decided to take the safe path and stay in the Atlanta suburbs, our lives would not be as rich today. When the chance comes, take a deep breath, measure the risks, decide as a team, and then jump with an explorer's attitude. Minimize the risk by speaking to a lot of people—on both sides of the fence. We were fortunate that Mary's sister, Nancy, lived in Seattle, so we had some family relatively close by. The worst thing that could have happened would have been that Yakima turned out to be horrible, but we got to spend some valuable time with Nancy after previously only seeing her at Christmas every other year with the occasional mid-year visit.

WHAT I LEARNED

Where you grow up does not determine your lifestyle for the rest of your life—good or bad. If you get the wandering spirit when you're young, give moving a try! What's the worst thing that can happen? You end up moving back to where you started, but you'll move back with life experiences that wouldn't have happened if you hadn't given it a chance. It also keeps you from wondering "what if" after you get older. Don't have a strict road map for your life. Know what you want, but be flexible along the way. For example, when Mary asked me if we should start trying to have children, I hadn't thought about that but said, "Sure!" Daniel and Caroline are the two miracles in our lives that have enriched us beyond belief.

I also learned the importance of moving as a team. When the job came up in Yakima, the company I went to work for paid for all of us to fly to Yakima since they believed the family was moving as much as the single employee. It was a huge statement. We voted at dinner one night and decided we should go for it. That decision changed the trajectory of our lives in so many ways. We had some challenging times, especially at the start, but we all decided to move, and we were all determined to enjoy it and make it work.

FIVE THOUGHTS TO HELP WHEN REMEMBERING FAMILY

1. If you move away, never forget where you came from—it had an impact.
2. Think of the people who sacrificed for you in early years.
3. Take a chance when a move comes up, but never forget your family is moving too.
4. If you move, dive into the local culture. Everyone will adapt quicker that way.
5. If, after giving it an honest try, the new place isn't for you, don't be afraid to make another move.

SUMMARY

"The root of joy is gratefulness."

— David Steindl-Rast

I'm extremely grateful for my family. Both the family I was born into and the family Mary and I created. Our family has been through many changes over the years, but the best experiences of our lives have been the result of taking chances, embracing change, and sticking together. I wouldn't be the person I am without my family. When I was growing up, my home life was positive and nurturing. After Mary and I married, even though we went through the normal family struggles, our home life resulted in all of us staying close.

I challenge you to remember your family and where you came from. Even if your family life was not ideal, use it to your benefit. I also challenge you to occasionally take a chance with your family. Deliberate together, come to a team decision, and then go for it!

CHAPTER 3

TRYING NEW THINGS AT ANY AGE

"You only live once, but if you do it right, once is enough."

— Mae West

What do you want your life to be? Have you ever had an epiphany when looking at your past that made you wonder, "What if I would have?" When I was forty-nine, I started thinking about how to celebrate turning fifty. It's a milestone year that can make people start to realize their mortality and try to plan how they might spend the rest of their days.

Critical points happen in life when you make decisions that will affect you for the rest of your life. For me, turning fifty was a big deal. I wanted to celebrate it in a way that appropriately marked the milestone. During the spring and summer of 2009, I started thinking hard about how I would mark the momentous occasion of turning fifty in November. Our daughter Caroline had just graduated from high school and would be leaving for the University of Washington in the fall. Our son Daniel was headed into his junior year of high school with plans to attend college. Because we raised our children to be independent, the chances were good that neither would be coming home to live after college.

At that time, I also read that fifty was a critical year for deciding which path you will go down for the rest of your life regarding your physical condition. Are you going to simply enjoy life, be a weekend athlete, struggle through the aches and pains that will come with that, get ready for retirement, and then cruise through the golden years? Or are you going to be disciplined in starting down the path of regular exercise to maintain muscle tone, eat healthier, stretch, think more about how you treat your body, and position yourself to be in good physical condition as you headed into the next phase of life?

I decided on the latter. I wanted to position myself to enjoy physical challenges later in life. I didn't have anything specific in mind like running a marathon or participating in a triathlon, but I decided if I wanted to do something physically challenging, I would be in good enough shape to start a more regimented training program. Then I wouldn't have to cope with the significant down time that would come with battling age and avoiding injury. I needed something to motivate me to get into good physical condition.

Once there, I would maintain a healthy schedule and regular routine. I needed a goal that would force me to train hard. It had to be lofty enough that I would stick with the training routine when I was traveling for work or life got in the way and my mind would inevitably say, "You don't need to work out today. Take the day off." It needed to be something so monumental that it would cause a lifestyle change.

You cannot avoid seeing mountains when you live in the Northwest—BIG mountains. Mount Rainier looms over you during a clear day in Seattle or when driving around the state. Mount Adams stared at me every day when I left our home to go to work. Mount Hood calls to you when you drive to Portland. I had never considered climbing a mountain when I lived in the Eastern US. Mountain climbing just seemed too out there for a regular guy who had grown up in a city where the only exposure was seeing people climb Mount Everest in a documentary. Regular people didn't climb mountains.

However, a guy in our office at Tree Top, Inc. (where I worked) had climbed mountains, and he seemed somewhat normal. Pete Shepard and I became friends in the office largely because we both had a somewhat practical, sarcastic sense of humor. I was in sales at Tree Top, and Pete ran the supply chain team. I would regularly run things by him in advance of sales presentations to get the other-side-of-the-desk perspective before meeting with customers. Pete was candid, smart, and able to explain his perspective in clear, concise terms. We also had quite a few laughs because of our similar senses of humor.

Pete seemed like a fitness fanatic—he was a big road biker, he walked a respectable distance from his home to work every day, and he was generally fit. Whenever I met with Pete in his office, I could look over his shoulders and see a print of the major Pacific Northwest mountains. Mount Rainier, Mount Hood, Mount Adams, and Mount St. Helens looked both menacing and mesmerizing. If you looked hard enough, you could also see Mount Jefferson way in the distance behind all four. One day, Pete and I somehow got into a discussion about mountains and mountain climbing.

Pete shared that he had climbed Mount Rainier and had attempted to summit Mount Denali in Alaska but was turned back because of complications caused by altitude sickness. The way he described the experiences was invigorating. I soon learned numerous people in the office and in the Northwest had either climbed or attempted to climb Mount Rainier. Normal people like me! While watching ESPN one day, I saw a story about NFL Commissioner Roger Goodell climbing Mount Rainier with Jim Mora (an NFL coach who had lived in the Pacific Northwest). Pictures were shown of the two of them on the summit. Now, Roger Goodell has a lofty position as NFL commissioner, but he never struck me as someone who had superior athletic ability. I decided if he could reach the top of Mount Rainier, so could I.

In the summer of 2009, while attending a corporate outing at a minor league baseball game in Yakima, I asked Pete Shepard what would be involved in climbing Mount Rainier. I don't remember the specific details, but his answer included that I should train in the hills just outside Yakima in Naches. He went on to be more specific and stated that when I could hike up Mount Cleman (Cot's Peak) and back to the car in two-and-a-half hours from the trailhead at the goat-feeding station, I would be ready to climb Mount Rainier. He also stated it would be best to go with one of the guide companies that climbed Mount Rainier.

Pete added that he had been thinking of climbing Mount Rainier again, so he would be happy to train with me, and he would research climbing guide companies so we could have the best chance of success. We could target the following summer to do the climb. That would give us enough time to train and see if I could get into the necessary physical shape.

After a few months, I went out to where I thought Pete had directed—Mount Cleman. I parked at the goat-feeding station just east of where Highways 12 and 410 intersected. I then proceeded to climb straight up the hill immediately in front of the parking lot. It was a tough haul over loose rocks without any signs of a trail. After a couple of hours of scrambling up loose rock, both upright and on my hands and knees, I reached the top of the peak with slightly bloody elbows and knees, took a picture, and sent it to Pete. His response, "Where are you?" When I described where I was, he asked if I had issues going over the stream. When I replied, "What stream?" I knew I was in the wrong place. While Pete had given good directions, I had forgotten the part to follow the goat trail to the right, over the stream and across the front of the mountain, and then make a hard left up Mount Cleman. In my excitement to get started, I had forgotten key parts of the directions. *Guess I'm going to need to listen better if I'm going to do this mountain climbing thing*, I thought. That was in the fall of 2009.

Mount Cleman is located just outside the small town of Naches, Washington. To reach the top (the metal Cot's Peak sign) entails hiking up almost 3,000 vertical feet over the distance of two miles. The grade varies between 11 and 42 percent. Doing the Waterworks Canyon (a longer route that starts just off Highway 410, down the road from the goat-feeding station) to Cleman is an eight-mile, 3,400-foot vertical gain. It's an up-and-down, strenuous hike that averages almost six hours to complete. The views from the top are spectacular! At the highest point on the Waterworks to Cleman hike, you can see the top of Mount Rainier as well as the patchwork quilt of orchards in the Yakima Valley.

In spring, when the apple trees are alive with white blooms, and in the fall, when the trees change color, the views are beyond description. That's the good part. However, the hike can also be extremely grueling. The vertical gain happens quickly, causing your heart to throb until it catches up to the pace you're going. Your calves burn on the way up, and the front of your thighs burn when you're descending. It's the perfect place to train in pursuit of a successful summit of Mount Rainier.

My first attempt at hiking to the top of Cot's Peak and back to the car took almost four hours—my thighs hurt for a week. If I were going to climb Mount Rainier successfully, I needed to do more than just hike. So, I started a regular gym routine of long cardio sessions on an elliptical machine; forty-five minutes with an average heart rate of 150 beats per minute, three times a week, along with push-ups and planks at least four times per week. This routine continued until early winter before the first snow fell. Then I started it up again in late winter when the snow cover was light enough to hike without slipping. The gym sessions went through the winter, and my cardio was maintained by skiing most weekends.

It's worth noting here that I'd already had some health issues I could have used as an excuse to stay sedentary. In my early forties, I was diagnosed with PFO (patent foramen ovale). PFO is a hole that develops in the heart after birth when the heart doesn't close the way it should after birth. Approximately one in four people have this condition. The hole is a small flaplike opening between the upper heart chambers. Usually, it goes undetected. Most people never need treatment. I only found out about the hole because of a very minor stroke I had in my early forties. I refused to let the diagnosis slow me down or stop me from pursuing my goals.

Once I started my hiking sessions in late winter, Pete and I would meet at the goat-feeding station and then hike to the top of Cot's Peak every Saturday or Sunday. Most times, we were joined by his son, Josh. Although painful, with all of us ending up a dirty sweaty mess, these sessions were tons of fun. Pete and Josh were significantly better hikers than me—usually hiking way ahead of me—but our sense of camaraderie and team spirit was refreshing. Pete always had positive coaching comments, even though he and Josh reached the top way in advance of me and returned to the car while I was still descending.

At the top of Cot's Peak, we would usually take a short snack and water break before heading back down to the car. After a few months of the training routine, it was time to choose a guide company that would get us to the top of Rainier. Because of their success rate, we chose IMG (International Mountain Guides). Their owners, George Dunn and Phil Erschler, had not only summitted Rainier hundreds of times but also had climbed Mount Everest. That convinced us they were the perfect company to go with. They also had an extra-acclimatization camp at the Ingraham Flats, increasing our chance of success. We chose a three-day trip that would put us at the summit in early July 2010 and promptly paid the down-payment. This was really going to happen!

As we trained over the next few months, I started purchasing the necessary gear suggested on the IMG website at REI (Recreational Equipment, Inc.). The necessities included an ice ax, crampons, harness, hard shell, soft shell, glissading pants, and glacier goggles. All the items were mentioned casually on the list, but I had never heard of most of them. What was a crampon anyway? Soon, I was a regular shopper at the REI store in Seattle and had completed acquiring the equipment I would need to climb Mount Rainier. By the time June came around, I could easily accomplish the conditioning goal Pete had set—up and down Mount Cleman, car to car in two-and-a-half hours. This training routine was working.

Mount Rainier's summit sits at an altitude of 14,441 feet (4,402 meters). It is the highest mountain in the state of Washington, is located fifty-nine miles southeast of Seattle, and is the most glaciated peak in the contiguous US. Due to its high probability of eruption soon and proximity to a major urban area, it is considered one of the world's most dangerous volcanoes. The National Park Service states that about 10,000 people attempt to climb Mount Rainier each year; only 50 percent succeed. Most attempt the summit via the Disappointment Cleaver-Ingraham Glacier route, located just after passing Camp Muir. (Yup, Disappointment Cleaver is a real name.) Some people also summit via the Emmons Glacier route with a stopover at Camp Sherman.

Climbing Mount Rainier is a significant challenge that shouldn't be taken lightly. Many marathon runners and triathletes fail to summit because of the unique training necessary and because they underestimate how severely altitude sickness can affect even the most well-conditioned athlete. To summit Mount Rainier via the Disappointment Cleaver route that Pete and I had decided on requires a start at the Paradise Parking lot in Mount Rainier National Park (where the visitors station is located) at an altitude of 5,400 vertical feet (1,646 meters). The grueling three-day, fifteen-mile trek involves a vertical gain of just over 9,000 feet (2,743 meters) in an effort to reach the 14,411-foot summit.

"Going to the mountains is going home."

— John Muir

Camp Muir, located at 10,000 feet (3,048 meters), is the approximate halfway point and where most people spend their first night. However, altitude sickness is known to affect people at this height, so it must be approached slowly to acclimatize correctly. From there, the fun gets technical. Because you will be on a glacier from Camp Muir to the summit, you're required to be on a rope team for safety reasons (to prevent you from falling into one of the many 1,000-foot (305 meters) or deeper crevasses or sliding down the steep mountainside to your death. From Camp Muir, the trail ascends quickly to the Ingraham Flats and then straight up Disappointment Cleaver to the summit of Mount Rainier. Pete and I continued to train hard in advance of our climb. We felt strong, and our confidence level was high.

Life has its twists and turns, though. In the spring of 2010, Mary's dad was diagnosed with bone cancer. Around the same time, my mom was diagnosed with lung cancer. We were scheduled to start our climb on July 6. On June 14, 2010, Mary's dad passed away in Atlanta. The death of a parent, especially one as physically fit as her dad, was a dose of reality that struck us hard. One week later, June 23, 2010, my mom died from her cancer after a hard-fought battle. Even though the deaths were expected, having two of our parents die within the span of a week created an emotional upheaval in our family. Mary was on the tarmac in Atlanta on her way home to Yakima when we found out my mom had died. Grieving two parents from both sides of our family at the same time is a circumstance few can understand.

In addition to all this happening, our climb date was rapidly approaching. My dad emphasized that I still needed to follow through with the climb, despite our family losses. Finally, the day came to make the drive to Ashland, Washington, and start our adventure at the IMG headquarters. On July 6, we started our hike up to Camp Muir where we would spend the first night of our journey. Over the next couple of days, we would learn the necessary emergency self-arrest skills that would potentially save our lives if we slid during our ascent. Then we roped up to go onto the glacier.

When we set out for Camp 2 on the Ingraham Glacier, Pete and I were feeling great, with no signs of altitude sickness. As we hiked up to the ridge (now as part of a rope team), where we would pass on our way to the Ingraham Glacier, we passed by a steep rock face on a snowfield with rocks exploding because of the freeze/thaw process at the higher levels. Boulders the size of large cars rolled down close to the trail we were on. The guides, in their calm deliberate voices, directed us to keep up a quick pace in the event any boulders rolled farther and caused injury. This was getting serious!

After passing through the snowfield, we made the ascent up the steep incline to the Cathedral Rocks Ridge. At the top of the ridge, the view took my breath away. There before me lay the Ingraham Flats, including the Ingraham Glacier, with a deep chasm just below where we would sleep that night, and just above, Little Tahoma, a steeply spiked mountain that is the third-highest peak in Washington. Until that point, I had only seen crevasses, glaciers, and Little Tahoma in pictures. To see them in real life gave me a sense of awe, and it immediately drove home both how serious this climb was and what an awesome, mind-blowing experience alpine climbing can be.

We made it to our campsite on the glacier, unloaded our packs and sleeping gear in the tent, and grabbed dinner. After going to bed early (before dark), we arose at 11 p.m., grabbed some breakfast, and then started hiking at 12:30 a.m. on July 8 to start our summit attempt. We left at 12:30 a.m. so we could hike on solid frozen snow to prevent us from falling into a crevasse and so our crampons got a good grip. If we had hiked this during the day, the danger level would have increased dramatically. I had barely slept the night before. After training week after week for nine months, we were about to head to the top of Mount Rainier. Both Pete and I were still feeling strong and anxious to get started. We climbed up the avalanche-prone slopes of Disappointment Cleaver, which included steep inclines of fifty degrees. Pete and I continued to check in with each other as we slowly ascended toward the top with our guide and the two other members of our rope team. Pete's conditioning routine had prepared us perfectly for this day.

We laughed regularly, and while sitting during a break at about 12,500 feet (3,810 meters), we marveled at the beauty of the magnificent sunrise unfiltered by the ground clouds. All was going smoothly until about 500 feet from the summit. I went to take a larger step when my mind went to my mom and how she was no longer around. A flood of emotions caused me to lose pace with my power breaths to keep my blood oxygen level higher to prevent altitude sickness. Power breaths are a helpful way to breathe when hiking at a high altitude. The procedure entails inhaling, then exhaling all of the air as hard and completely as possible. It allows you to get the oxygen you need, but it also quickly pushes out the carbon dioxide.

Suddenly, without warning, I experienced tunnel vision, nausea, and a dull headache that wouldn't go away. We pressed on and cleared the crater rim at around 6 a.m. The emotional wave hit me hard all at once. Here we were at the summit of Mount Rainier, which I had seen from afar for the past four years, and trained hard for nine months to ascend. Now, thinking of my mom and her influence on my life, I cried like a baby, then screamed out in victory as we passed the crater rim. At that point, the altitude sickness returned with a splitting headache, and I thought I was going to throw up. I told Pete to go on without me since I could see in his eyes that he was aching to get to the true summit—Columbia Crest located on the other side of the crater about a mile away.

One of the guides noticed I was struggling, so he came over to ask how he could help. He informed me that since we had summitted, I didn't need to go all the way over to Columbia Crest. I wanted no part of that. "I don't know when I'll be back here again," I told him. We started walking toward Columbia Crest in a slow, deliberate fashion, one step at a time, while continually taking deep power breaths. During that walk, he told me of his background as a soldier in the British Special Forces. He also said studies have shown that when an average person feels physically spent while doing a strenuous activity, they are at only 40 percent of their max capacity. That's all I needed to hear—I still had some gas in the tank. I met up with Pete on top of Columbia Crest, the true summit of Mount Rainier, at around 7 a.m. on a crystal-clear, royal-blue-sky morning on July 9, 2010. All the painful morning hikes and strenuous workouts had been well worth it.

Words cannot properly express the emotions I experienced that day. It was the pinnacle of realizing a goal met after months of training. Over the past month, I had experienced extreme sadness by going to two funerals for parents. Now, I felt unfathomable elation, gratitude, pride, and a strong sense of accomplishment while standing on top of that mountain. I experienced the highest high from any athletic activity I had done. As I later said in an interview, "Other than the birth of my children and the marriage to my wife, this was the most impactful event of my life."

Shortly after summiting, we headed back down to our high camp, then past Camp Muir, and to the parking lot at Paradise and the visitors center. On the way down from the summit, it's numbing to see what you didn't see in the dark on the way up. During our descent, the small cracks in the ice and the walkways we traveled over in the dark were exposed in the light. Looking below us while we walked in the light, you could see the depth of the huge crevasses—sometime thousands of feet deep. Most of the openings were so deep that the colors were a deep shade of blue that gradually turned into a black abyss.

While Pete and I sat on the ground waiting for the shuttle to take us back to the IMG headquarters in Ashland, I expressed my gratitude for all the time he had spent getting us ready to tackle this unbelievable feat. If not for him, I doubt I would have known where to start in my efforts to properly train or what to expect along the way. Little did he know he had started me on a path that would change me forever.

WHAT I LEARNED

Have you ever set a lofty goal and didn't know exactly how you would achieve it? Did you put your faith in someone helping you to get there? I didn't really know what to expect during my first big mountain climb. When we reached the crater rim, I was shocked to learn we would not be putting a stake in the ground like Hillary did on Mount Everest. Instead, we would bathe in the beautiful sunshine in a live volcanic crater, where I could see the hissing steam coming out of vents that went deep into the volcano's belly.

While I had read some books about the topic beforehand, feeling the elation of success was a one-of-a-kind experience. I learned that if you break a challenge down into pieces and you dream big, remarkable things can happen. During our eight-month training routine, I had experienced extreme pain, enjoyed stunning surroundings, and developed a bond with a new friend that's hard to explain. Pete and I would not have become friends if not for the Rainier experience. Over that training period, I had lost about thirty pounds and got into the best shape of my life at a stage when some people start heading downhill toward a sedentary life. My birthday celebration had achieved its goal. I am grateful to Pete for taking me under his wing.

FIVE THOUGHTS ON TRYING NEW THINGS AT ANY AGE

1. If you think of something to do that's outrageous—no matter what your age—give it a whirl.
2. Find someone you trust who can show you how to achieve the goal.
3. When you choose to do extreme things in later life, come up with a plan.
4. A plan is good—prepare yourself to be surprised and adjust.
5. Enjoy the victory!

SUMMARY

"The greatest danger for most of us is not that our aim is too high and we miss it, but that it is too low and we reach it."

— Michelangelo

So, what is your challenge to yourself? It doesn't need to be to climb a mountain, but it can be something you think is impossible. I challenge you to run that 5k, 10k, or marathon you've been eyeing. I challenge you to hike the Appalachian Trail. I challenge you to hike the Pacific Crest Trail. Give it a shot! If this flatlander Philly boy can make it to the top of an iconic mountain, you can reach a summit you never thought you could. Go crush it!

CHAPTER 4

SAYING GOODBYE MIGHT BE FOREVER

"The past is frozen and no longer flows, and
the present is all lit up with eternal rays."

— C.S. Lewis

We all say goodbye to people we expect to see again soon. But what if you said goodbye, only to never see or speak to them again? Would you have said something differently? Would you have hugged a few seconds longer?

When I dropped Mary off at the Salt Lake City airport after Caroline's wedding in June 2022, it was the only time I said goodbye when I thought the chance existed that we might not see each other again. Let me go back a little.

Caroline and I had experienced several adventures over the years, including numerous mountain-climbing experiences. She was the person I had climbed my second mountain with—Mount Adams. She was the one who went crevasse climbing with me when we spent the day with Foursquare Mountaineering, a climbing club based in Yakima, at the Nisqually Glacier on Mount Rainier. She was the one who pushed us to climb Mount Whitney—and then go to Death Valley to experience the highest and lowest elevations in the contiguous United States in two days. She was the one who immediately said, "I'm in" when I started planning our trip to climb Mount Kilimanjaro. We were and still are friends who share a sense of adventure and are big planners.

When Caroline and her fiancé Anthony Hernandez decided to get married outside of Park City at the High West Distillery, no one was more thrilled than I was. They chose that location because of the great memories the two of them had of Utah and Park City since that's where they had met. Utah has boundless beauty—tall mountains, vast open spaces, and great trails to hike and bike. Since starting my climbing voyage, I, too, had great memories of Utah. Caroline and I had annual father/daughter weekends there over the years while she worked for Goldman Sachs. We hiked together to some taller peaks and skied a variety of the resorts. It was almost like our special place. During one of those trips, we decided not to ski and instead visit the High West Distillery outside of Park City in Wanship, Utah. The views from the back of their property were stunning. While there aren't any dramatic peaks, the significant rolling hills in this rural part of eastern Utah make it an outdoor person's dream. When Caroline and Anthony chose their wedding date in late June, it seemed like it would be the perfect time of year.

Once they had settled on the date, I started thinking about taking advantage of the trip out there by pondering which peaks could be climbed after the wedding. It sounded like the perfect plan—have the wedding, celebrate a momentous family event, send them off, and then go hike or climb with some friends. Mark McGuire, a member of our climbing club, had moved to Bozeman a few years earlier, and Jim Zingerman, a member of Foursquare Mountaineering, Mark, and I had skied in the area during the winter a few times. They are almost always up for an adventure, so I thought it would be perfect. The three of us could find something to climb in the area after the wedding. We decided to climb the Grand Teton. I felt comfortable with the decision and that I could compartmentalize the two events; concentrate on the wedding on the front end of the trip, then start focusing on a climb after Caroline and Anthony headed out on their honeymoon. Good plan, right?

Watching my baby girl get married was a more moving experience than I had expected. The emotional part resulted from how she would now be transitioning from her role as daughter to that of wife. My status in her life was about to decrease, but I was comfortable with that. I couldn't have wished for a better life partner for her. Anthony is a great guy; he's hard-working, respects my daughter, and has never tried to quell her sense of adventure or her aspiring spirit. After all, once Caroline decides to do something, she will find a way to do it, and my respect for her determination is immense.

The wedding day was perfect, and everything went off without a hitch. Although people asked me about the upcoming climb, I remained in the moment.

After we said goodbye to Caroline and Anthony, I started thinking about my next adventure, climbing the Grand Teton. I had beefed up my usual workout routine in advance of the trip and felt good about the climb. However, for some reason, the wedding had put thoughts of my mortality in mind. In the past, I had gone off on hikes and high-altitude climbs without any thought of not coming back. Now, something inside me cried out that I make certain Mary know that if I did not make it back, she should delay telling Caroline until she got home from her overseas honeymoon. The request was unusual and unfair.

Why did I make the request? Was it because I didn't want an event outside of Caroline's control to put a cloud over the best event in her life? Or was it the potential embarrassment of coming up short in the eyes of my daughter whom I had so much respect for? I don't know why I said it, but it freaks me out that I must have had a premonition of the accident that was to be so life-threatening.

"Nature's peace will flow into you as sunshine flows into the trees."

— John Muir

The other time saying goodbye for the last time came to light for me was when I said goodbye to my best friend, Pete Matheson, at the end of a phone call on August 12, 2017, at 9:47 a.m. EST. Pete and I became friends soon after I moved to Yakima because our wives were in a coffee group together. At first, our relationship was casual, but then it bloomed into a brotherly bond out of respect for each other and a desire to make each other better while having loads of fun. Along with Pete's wife, Donna, we had the rare experience of having a couples' relationship where everyone got along extremely well. The four of us had a blast together, and we all fed off each other's desire to enjoy life. Pete was like my dad in so many ways: He was one of the hardest-working people I had ever known; he had a larger-than-life personality that could light up a room; he believed in strong family values; and he never had a hard time expressing his emotions. We had one of those once-in-a-lifetime friendships not everyone gets to experience. We were blessed.

I got Pete into alpine climbing after I had been doing it for a couple of years. Basically, Pete loved hard work. His determination to undertake difficult things, love of the outdoors, and desire to train hard in advance made him perfect for the sometimes grueling mental and physical stamina you need to accomplish climbing goals and push yourself beyond what you thought you could do. While many, including me, think training is a chore, Pete practically thrived on the pain involved and always had a big smile while sopping wet from sweat. During our Saturday morning, four-hour-plus training hikes in the hills outside of Naches, Washington, we laughed, anguished, and shared our thoughts on life, our career, and our families (past and present), and generally passed the time experiencing one of the rare joys people get to experience—true friendship. Pete kept me accountable and wasn't afraid of jeopardizing our relationship to make me a better person.

Those training hikes with Pete were remarkable. I told my son Daniel that the move to Yakima was one of the best things that had happened to me because of my friendship with Pete. We climbed Mount Adams numerous times with the climbing club and included our sons. Even our children got along well!

Since Pete grew up outside of Chicago, he was blown away by all the huge mountains in Washington and their stunning natural beauty. Although Pete was a high-level executive in his company, he was the humblest when climbing with the club. Our weekend trips to the top of Mount Adams, Mount St. Helens, Mount Stuart, Colchuck Peak, and Ingles Peak, to name a few, are burned in my memory as monumental life experiences, largely due to the camaraderie the climbing club offered, but also because Pete came along with his always positive outlook, candid comedic remarks, and make-it-happen mentality. Pete's desire to climb Mount Rainier was insatiable. We had plans to climb Mount Rainier together with the climbing club, but unfortunately, he had to turn back because of exhaustion and altitude sickness.

Because of a job opportunity, Mary and I moved back to Atlanta in the spring of 2017. Life isn't always fair. We moved while thinking we would go back and forth, with Donna and Pete visiting us in Atlanta and us regularly visiting them in Yakima. When we moved on March 17, we knew our bond would sustain a move. Pete summited Mount Rainier in the spring of 2017 (after I moved) with the Yakima Climbing Club. Hearing his voice and his sense of pride and accomplishment brought tears to my eyes when we talked on the phone after he got back home. I was so happy for him and proud of what my friend had accomplished after years of training.

After summiting Rainier, Pete and I decided it would be fun to climb Mount Whitney with our children. He would climb with his son Joe; I would climb with my daughter Caroline. At 14,505 feet, Mount Whitney is the tallest mountain in the contiguous United States (Mount Denali in Alaska, formerly known as Mount McKinley, is the tallest peak on the North American continent). While many people hike Mount Whitney in a day, it's a bit of an extreme endurance push. The climb involves starting in the morning a few hours before sunrise to get on the trail and hike the twenty-two-mile-round-trip trail to the top where you will gain almost 7,000 feet of elevation. While the hike through the woods is beautiful, once you leave the forest, you enter a rocky/barren environment and then hike up ninety-nine switchbacks (the trail going back and forth like a Z to gain gradual elevation). I thought they were kidding when they said there were ninety-nine; they weren't!

We started training for the hike up the tallest peak in the continental US right away and compared training notes regularly, even though I was in Atlanta. We were having one of those phone discussions before his training hike up Cot's Peak outside of Naches, Washington. When we hung up the phone that Saturday morning, we said our goodbyes in the usual fashion. Later that morning, things would go terribly wrong. During his training hike, Pete fell a significant distance off a ledge. Mary and I were at a wedding in Atlanta when I started to get text messages that Pete was missing. After Donna called members of the climbing club, they went looking for him. They later told me the winds had significantly increased and he had not come home, even after dark. Knowing how strong and invincible he was, I just knew Pete had hunkered down somewhere with his jar of pickle juice (he always carried some to reduce muscle cramping) and was waiting for the right time to appear.

The next day, Donna informed us Pete had fallen and died as a result. I experienced a combination of disbelief, shock, despair, depression, and extreme sadness. It was one of the lowest points of my life. Life doesn't give you do-overs. If I had known how fleeting those spectacular times together with Pete would be, I'm not sure I would have moved back to Atlanta. While I didn't get to let Pete know how much our friendship meant to me before we hung up the phone that morning, I take comfort in knowing we had communicated that regularly. Fortunately, Donna and her and Pete's sons, Joe and William (along with William's wife Jordan), are now and will always be part of our family. The bond we share and the times we all spend together keep Pete close to us, even though we all miss him deeply. We continue to always have "just another splash" in Pete's honor during our get-togethers.

WHAT I LEARNED

"Here today and gone tomorrow" is a phrase that's bounced around at various times. While it applies to many things, it definitely applies to the times we spend with friends and family. We don't get any do-overs. Since no one gets a peek at where and when they will die, it's best to say goodbye in a way that leaves no guessing about how much someone means to you if they have a special place in your heart.

FIVE THOUGHTS ABOUT HOW SAYING GOODBYE MIGHT BE FOREVER

1. Stay in the moment and enjoy what you are doing *today*.
2. Take time to realize you're spending time with special friends while you're with them.
3. Real friends are rare to come by, so cherish them!
4. Say goodbye like it might be forever.
5. Remember, we don't always get do-overs.

SUMMARY

"Mindfulness is simply being aware of what is happening right now without wishing it were different."

— James Baraz

So, how do you avoid remorse if you see someone for the last time? Say goodbye as if it's the last time—not in a sad way, but in a happy way that makes certain if it is the last time, it wasn't taken for granted and so you can visualize that tight hug or warm handshake. While I still make the mistake of not applying this lesson learned all the time, I do so more often. That's also why when I said goodbye to Mary at the Salt Lake City airport, I wanted to communicate a specific message so there would not be any doubt of what to do if something tragic happened. When I said goodbye to Pete that morning on August 12, I'm glad we said goodbye laughing about something stupid.

I challenge you to think about your goodbyes. I challenge you to say goodbye and hug tighter, shake hands warmer, and do so with meaning. I challenge you to say goodbye like it might be the last time, and to make it a good memory until you see someone again...hopefully.

CHAPTER 5

MAKING FRIENDS FOR LIFE

"Many people will walk in and out of your life, but
only true friends will leave footprints in your heart."

— Eleanor Roosevelt

Have you ever looked back on some friendships and wondered how someone from such a different background with a different personality and some diverging viewpoints could have such a deep personal relationship with you? True friendships are few and far between. We have many acquaintances as we go through life, but we only have a few people we know who, even though we don't talk often, if we call them, the fires of our friendship reignite. Foursquare Mountaineering, the core Yakima climbing group that welcomed me into their circle, is one group of people I know will be in my friends-for-life club. I look back and wonder how such a diverse group could have ever spent so much time together, laughed hard at so many things (including each other), and had conversations that went on for hours without end while we experienced pushing ourselves to extremes. All this without any internal bickering—except when we were "slightly misdirected" on the trail.

My plan with Mount Rainier was for it to be a one-and-done experience. It would get me to where I wanted to be health-wise. Then I would find something else to tackle in efforts to remain in the same physical condition. I never thought I would climb another mountain. But soon after climbing Mount Rainier, our neighbor Diane introduced her new husband, David Stoothoff, to Mary and me. While we chatted, I started a side conversation with David. Soon the conversation circled around climbing Mount Rainier. I shared with Dave that I had climbed Mount Rainier the previous summer. He shared that he, too, had been to the top of Mount Rainier, and he was in a regular hiking and climbing club. They had an annual trip up Mount Adams in June, and he suggested I come along.

Foursquare Mountaineering, the Yakima climbing club I soon became a member of, was a group of guys who all belonged to the Foursquare Church in Yakima and had a passion for hiking challenging mountains on the weekends. The original group of guys I was exposed to included Doug White, Mark McGuire, Dave Stoothoff, Jim Zingerman, Dennis Elliott, and Ron Cowan. They were a diverse group from a variety of occupations who had strong religious convictions, were humble, and had a drive to hike challenging mountains on the weekends. Even though they are reserved and steady, they are some of the toughest guys I have known, both physically and mentally.

Mark McGuire and Doug White, who were somewhat the ad hoc leaders, had the most technical experience and were considered the strongest climbers in the group. They had earned the group's respect because of their remarkable physical stamina, along with their daring escapades while alpine climbing and rock climbing throughout the Pacific Northwest.

If you judged Doug's capacity for climbing based on his size and you thought you could outpace him, you were in for a rude awakening and a painful experience. While on the smaller side, Doug would carry fifty-to-sixty-pound packs with ease. He also was one of the quickest hikers and climbers, often setting a pace that would drain you if you tried to keep up. While a good conversationalist, he was quiet, direct, and deliberate. Doug had a wealth of knowledge of the surrounding mountains and trails, in addition to technical climbing knowledge because of his rock-climbing background. Because of his mental and physical stamina, knowledge, and tenacity, Doug was a guy you always wanted on a challenging climb. He usually organized our weekend adventures, laid out the path we would take, and then led us to our destination. He was a remarkable leader.

Dennis Elliott was our resident sixties guy, complete with his signature ponytail. Although Dennis had spent some time in a motorcycle club in California, he was a calm and gentle soul. He worked as a machinist by trade and worked on motorcycles. Dennis was a giving soul who exemplified what a true Christian should be; he lived his faith and was a testimony to a calm, godly spirit. His temperament was even more remarkable because his son had been severely wounded during the war in Iraq. Dennis had made many trips back east to visit his son while he recovered. You never heard him complain or give the "Woe is me" speech. When anyone asked how his son was, Dennis always told us how great he was recovering. In fact, his son eventually became a respected paralympic skier. Whenever you met Dennis, he always gave you a warm hug, warm smile, and a greeting that made you feel special. Being from Philadelphia and constantly in a professional environment, I had never been around huggers other than family members. I hadn't been exposed to openly warm guys who greeted you so sincerely.

Dennis was another one in the club whose strength you could easily misjudge because of his slender build. He could hike and climb with the best of them. On one trip up Mount Adams, a guy got so exhausted that he just laid his pack on the trail and continued hiking without it to our camping location. When Dennis heard this, he trekked back down the trail, after setting up his camp, helped the guy look for his pack, and allowed him to share his tent. Dennis exemplified someone who would give you the shirt off his back if you were in need.

My neighbor Dave Stoothoff was another of the gentle spirits, who was part of Foursquare Mountaineering. Dave worked for the City of Yakima. His soothing voice disarmed situations regularly. He was very open about his love of God and how much he depended on his faith. He regularly praised God for the beauty that surrounded us on our trips. In addition to the training hikes the group would do on weekends (and sometimes during the week), Dave and I would regularly "hike the hill" behind our homes in West Valley—a rural section west of downtown Yakima. We would meet up in Dave's driveway, hike up the paved driveway that would lead to an orchard, and then cut through the orchard and over a fence, and get in a heart-thumping thousand feet or so climb in efforts to train.

Although the hikes would last a few hours, the time flew by quickly because of the interesting conversations we would have about his large extended family and how he grew up in rural areas of Washington. Dave loved the outdoors—especially the state of Washington. He told me God had created Washington by combining the best parts of each of the other states. He had an even pace when hiking and was the example of slow and steady wins the race, both when training and when we were on our adventures. Dave also taught me to take the time to enjoy the hike instead of just plowing your way to the top. Although we jabbed him about always wanting to "take some pictures" of flowers and trees along the way so he could remember the beauty we were hiking through, I think each of us wished we had a little bit of Dave in us so we could better savor the experience. Since I'm someone always in a hurry to get places, it was great hiking with Dave because of his calm demeanor.

Ron Cowan came from one of the apple-growing families in the Yakima Valley. Caroline and I got to know him and his daughter during our first climb up Mount Adams together. Because of his connection with his daughter, we immediately hit it off. Ron is also someone who doesn't get frazzled when things get edgy. On one climb up to Three Finger Lookout in the North Cascades (more about that later), my high regard for Ron and his resilient toughness increased. The year prior, Ron had been diagnosed with cancer. He took the entire year off to heal while he received treatments. The Three Finger Lookout hike consists of a long mountain bike ride, a significant hike, and then a steep climb up to a ranger lookout station. The adventure was the first climb he had been on since his illness. Even though it was a tough hike, Ron muscled through a very challenging trip without any complaints—taking in the adventure we were on with a big smile and positive attitude, even though I knew he was in a lot of pain from being unable to train in advance of the trip.

Pete Shepard joined the Foursquare club about the same time as me in the spring of 2011. Even though he joined the group as an outsider, like I did, he fit in perfectly with the group; a gutsy, strong hiker, he respected the people he was hiking with and enjoyed the challenge of doing something that pushed him.

Pete Matheson joined the group the following year in advance of our annual trip to climb Mount Adams. I told Pete he was perfect for this climbing environment since work was what he got the most enjoyment out of….and hard work was involved in this hobby.

Although Mark McGuire had been part of Foursquare Mountaineering long before I got involved, I didn't meet him until after hiking with the group for a season since he hadn't been as involved that year. Dave Stoothoff introduced us while skiing at White Pass, the ski area about forty-five minutes away from Yakima in the Cascade Mountains. Little did I know my climbing and outdoor activity level was about to take an exponential leap. Mark had taken up rock climbing early in his life. It was an activity he and his dad found they loved and could do together. Mark is probably the toughest person I know, both mentally and physically. His pain threshold is so high I sometimes wonder if he should be studied. If the study is correct that we are only at 40 percent when we hit our first state of exhaustion, Mark's 40 percent is probably equal to most people's 80 percent.

Mark and I skied together numerous times that winter, and we went on some of the Foursquare hikes and climbs the following summer and fall. Mark introduced me to the world of backcountry skiing the next winter. Once again, I was exposed to something I had not heard of or dreamed was possible. Backcountry skiing is when you have special boots and skis that allow you to walk up hills outside the boundaries of the ski area by adjusting your boots to a walk mode, and the boot heels can lift out of the bindings. It also requires you to put "skins" (nylon sheets, originally made from animal skins, that run the length of your skis) on the bottom of your skis. The skins work like reverse fish scales on the way up so you can walk with traction without sliding downhill. Climbing up mountainsides using skins on your skis is known as "skinning." The experience opened a whole new world to me. I had skied most of my life and regularly skied almost every weekend during the winter after we moved to Yakima. Skiing was always my go-to mind clearer because it forces you to be in the moment while being outside. Mark would take me out to an area known as "The Digit" because of how the vertical rock formation rose straight up into the air—like someone giving you the middle finger.

Not only was Mark the best skier I had seen inbounds, but he is also hands-down the best skier I have seen out of bounds. We would slide under the out-of-bounds ropes just above the top of the chairlift at White Pass, skin up to the ridge just below The Digit, and then spend the day skinning up and skiing down in virgin powder. The area was wild, untouched, quiet, and expansive. Most of the time, we were the only people out there. On Saturdays or Sundays, if we went backcountry skiing, we would spend the morning skinning up, then skiing down; stop to grab lunch at the top of a ride where the expanse of the Cascades went on forever without any human touch; and then spend the afternoon doing the same routine as the morning. Even though I was brand new to the experience and felt as though I was a fish out of water, Mark always had a positive comment. Once, when I had issues coming down a chute that made my butt pucker, he greeted me at the bottom of the chute with that sly smile and said, "You're doing great!"

At times, to get to the perfect skin area out of bounds, we had to carry our skis while hiking in thigh-deep snow. The physical exertion was extreme, but when you clicked into your skis again and swooshed down, it was like floating on air. Once the world of backcountry skiing was opened to me, the options became expansive. One memorable adventure was when Mark, Doug, and I decided to go to the top of Mount Hood, which looms at 11,249 feet just outside Portland, Oregon. Mark challenged me to try skinning up to the top and skiing down. Doug White planned on hiking to the top.

Unfortunately, because of icy conditions on the way up, I was forced to stash my skis partway and hike to the top with Doug White. The trip up Mount Hood ended up being one of the longest days of my life, but it taught me so many things, including asking a few more questions in advance, taking a descent slowly because of the steep pitch on the descent from the top, and that (because Mark was able to ski) some of the highest peaks in the area could be skied, even though they did not have accessibility by a chairlift—only by your bodily strength.

"Of all the paths you take in life, make sure a few of them are dirt."

— John Muir

That trip led to Mark and me hiking and skinning up to the recently erupted crater rim of Mount St. Helens in Washington. While I had been to the crater rim a few times, including on trips with my brother Dave, his wife Jan, and our nephew Ryan Simpson, and then again with Pete Matheson, I always find the place simply breathtaking. The exhilaration of clicking into bindings at the rim of a live volcano that is hissing and bubbling is mind-blowing. None of that would have happened without the tough love, "you can do anything you set your mind to" philosophy of Mark McGuire. For that, I am forever grateful.

Jim Zingerman was the final regular member of Foursquare Mountaineering group. A family doctor in Selah, Washington (just outside Yakima), I would describe Jim as the yin to my yang. While I can be impulsive and jump into things because they seem exciting without thinking it through, Jim is a cranial, calm spirit with a gentle voice who often asks, "Is that the wise decision?" Jim got into climbing the same way I did. Having grown up in New York, he had always enjoyed the outdoors, but he had not grown up experiencing the extremes of the Pacific Northwest like Doug, Mark, Dennis, and Ron had.

We also liked hiking and climbing together because our physical strength was similar, unlike Doug and Mark, who were superhuman. Jim is usually game for an adventure, but always after asking some questions and thinking it through. However, he's also been in the same situation as me where he's thought, *Should we really be here?*

Over the years, Jim and I have become close friends for a variety of reasons—mostly because we're the novices in the group, but also because a conversation with Jim makes you think. He's very open with his emotions without being emotional, and he has deep, clear religious convictions without evangelizing. He's also a matter-of-fact, caring person. One example is the time we took on the challenge to go to the top of the Three Finger Lookout one weekend.

The Three Finger Lookout challenge is a 31.5 mile/6,500-foot vertical gain in the North Cascades that was described in one outdoor magazine as a hike that "sounds like a shopping spree at REI." The experience requires a mountain bike, a backpack loaded with camping gear, crampons, an ice ax, and enough cold weather gear to keep you warm on a very exposed mountaintop. It starts with an eight-to-ten-mile mountain bike ride up a logging road with about a 1,400-foot vertical gain. Once you reach the trailhead, you lock your bike to a tree and start a gradual hike through the woods until you reach a beautiful meadow with a babbling stream. At that point, you get a look at the prize—a tiny, fire-lookout hut sitting atop a jagged mountain peak.

From there the trail gets steeper and steeper, culminating in a traverse across a steep snowfield to the base of a jagged spire. All told, the hike is around an additional seven-to-eight miles and 4,000-foot vertical gain from the time you leave your bike at the trailhead. Getting to the top entails climbing up a wobbly ladder and then scrambling, hand-over-hand, using a permanent knotted rope to get to the lookout station delicately perched on the top of a small landing that's held in place by multiple cables drilled into the rock. The view from the top is remarkable! You can see for miles to the east, deep into the North Cascades, then turn 180 degrees and see the Puget Sound off the coast of Washington. While it was a strenuous couple of days, we all agreed it was one of our most memorable experiences.

At the end of the two-day adventure, we arrived at our car at the trailhead, exhausted but ecstatic from the experience. We bragged, while taking off our hiking boots and changing clothes, that it was one of the few trips with no "incidents." About that time, a woman frantically came up to our car to ask for help; her dad had fallen down a waterfall while trying to take pictures. Jim is a doctor so he volunteered to go with her to see how he could help.

After evaluating the father, Jim decided he needed medical attention because of an obvious broken leg. Because we were out of cell phone range deep in the wilderness, we decided Jim would go with the woman and her dad in their car out to the main highway and call for an ambulance. It seemed like the right thing to do since we were still waiting for Dave to finish and could meet up with Jim out on the main road after the ambulance took the dad to the hospital. Only after we saw the car with Jim, the wounded man, and his daughter go out of sight did reality set in—we didn't know them and may have just sent our friend off to his demise with psychotic strangers. Oh, and the dad had a huge pistol strapped to his waist that he had said he carried for protection. The thought of danger had never entered Jim's mind.

Well, we eventually met up with Jim on the main highway; we were relieved to see him sitting by the side of the road in front of a bar waiting for us. He described the rest of the ordeal with the daughter and dad as not being ideal, with both acting nonsensically, including the dad stating he didn't need an ambulance when they got to the road. Jim explained the whole wacky situation to us in the same voice and cadence you would use to read a bedtime story to your grandchildren.

Between 2011 and 2016, our climbing club went on numerous adventures. We would meet in the early spring as a group and discuss what we planned on tackling that year. Then we put the plan into motion to climb various peaks throughout the Pacific Northwest. In preparation for our climbing season, we would regularly train by climbing to the top of Cot's Peak (Mount Cleman). Those training sessions in the hills outside of Naches hold great memories. Once, we organized an Easter sunrise service at Cot's Peak on Mount Cleman. Celebrating a religious event in such a way was not something I had done previously. We started early Easter morning in the dark and enjoyed the explosion of Easter morning while conducting a small Easter service together.

During my time with the climbing club, I had the chance to climb Mount Adams with Caroline; we got slightly lost and incorrectly used our ice axes on the descent (without injury). I also had an emotional experience summitting Mount Adams with Daniel while he was going through some challenging times. With Pete Matheson, I climbed and summitted Mount Stuart, Colchuck Peak, Ingles Peak, including Ingles Lake (one of the most beautiful places

I've experienced), Mount Adams, and Mount St. Helens. In addition, I had the chance to experience a skin/ski attempt of Mount Baker, I was exposed to one of the most stunning places in Washington—The Enchantments— and I climbed Dragon Tail Peak via Asgaard Pass. That climb ends with a stunning view of the turquoise-blue water of Colchuck Lake from the 9,000- foot jagged summit.

WHAT I LEARNED

Joining Foursquare Mountaineering was a pivotal point in my life in so many ways. It taught me that you can be open and comfortable talking about your faith with friends. Friendships, real friendships, can come at you unexpectedly. When they do, enjoy the ride because life changes quickly— sometimes planned, sometimes unexpectedly. While hiking and climbing with this group of guys, I was able to continue to push myself further than I ever dreamed possible, hitting the edge of sheer exhaustion. Such times with the club tested my mental and emotional limits.

FIVE THOUGHTS ABOUT FOREVER FRIENDS

1. Good friends can pop up anywhere, suddenly, and last forever.

2. Don't judge based on a first impression.

3. Sometimes letting the group take the lead is a good thing.

4. Real friends rally together during the lowest times.

5. The most-experienced people are usually the humblest.

SUMMARY

"I'm so glad you are here. It helps me realize how beautiful my world is."

— Rainer Maria Rilke

My experiences with these phenomenal guys included the exuberance that comes from setting lofty goals, working hard to prepare to achieve them, and then reaching the goal and the extreme emotional outburst that comes with it. We also experienced the extreme low of the guys looking for Pete Matheson for hours in extreme conditions—sometimes on their hands and knees because of the strong winds—only to learn the search and rescue team had found him unresponsive and realized he had died because of a fall. Most importantly, I learned a group of people from extremely diverse backgrounds and occupations could work together in extreme situations as a team, push ourselves to the edge, and experience unbounded happiness while creating a bond few people ever experience. These memories will stay in my heart forever.

I challenge you to find real friends. I challenge you to cultivate and nurture those relationships. Most importantly, I challenge you not to take the people you deeply connect with for granted.

CHAPTER 6

PREPARING FOR THE UNEXPECTED

"The difference between ordinary and
extraordinary is that little extra."

— Jimmy Johnson

Have you ever planned and planned for something, thinking you've taken everything into account, only to be surprised when you started on a journey? By nature, we try to control most things we get involved in. I've found that human nature leans toward people not wanting surprises. Surprises catch us off guard. The dictionary defines a surprise as feeling "mild astonishment or shock." Being caught off guard because of a "surprise party" is a pleasant surprise. However, when you're surprised by your surroundings, expecting one thing and then experiencing something completely different, it can really catch you off guard. Anyone who has spent any decent amount of time outdoors has been surprised when going on a hike, a backpacking trip, or climbing a mountain. The ten essentials (map, compass, sunglasses/sunscreen, extra clothing, headlamp/flashlight, first-aid supplies, fire starter, matches, knife, and extra food) for hiking are meant to prepare you for any surprises and unexpected turns when you're in the wild. Surprise! Being surprised is an inherent part of the game. But it's not the surprise that adds to the adventure; it's how you respond to it that can make the trip epic or a disaster.

Kilimanjaro was one climb where we encountered a big surprise. At 19,341 feet, it truly is an epic climb. Not only is the height spectacular, but it carries three unique titles that put it on many climbers and hikers' must-do lists. Mount Kilimanjaro is the tallest peak on the African continent. It is also the highest free-standing mountain in the world. When you set out to climb anything described as the "tallest," "most difficult," "longest," "in the world," it comes with a certain set of expectations and an ego feed. Add to the tallest the title of being one of the famed seven summits, the tallest peaks on each of the seven continents, and you have a challenge that gets people's hearts pumping and exciting expectations that come with a must-do goal.

Setting the goal of climbing Mount Kilimanjaro had been on my radar for a few years. At fifty, my goal was to climb Mount Rainier (which was supposed to be one and done). After climbing Mount Rainier and hiking several peaks with the Foursquare group, I decided it would be cool to do an epic climb every five years to celebrate milestone birthdays. Parties are fun, especially for birthdays after fifty. Setting lofty goals to celebrate the excitement of a milestone birthday instead of celebrating being "over the hill" for me is the way to go. If you say you're over the hill, you're telling the world your best days are in the past and it's all downhill from there.

Setting challenging goals to push yourself puts you in a completely different state of mind, one that believes "The best is yet to come" and thinks, *Why can't I do that?* I had planned to climb a different route up Mount Rainier for my fifty-fifth birthday in 2014. That plan changed when Pete Matheson and I set the goal to climb Mount Rainier—his first and my second time up—the year before I turned fifty-five. Oh well, doing the climb a year early, especially with my best friend, seemed like a good pivot. Once I turned fifty-five, I started thinking about the challenge I wanted to do at sixty. At that point, I started thinking about Mount Kilimanjaro. Based on my research, it seemed very doable, and because it was on the African continent—somewhere I had never thought about going—even more exciting!

I knew going all the way to Africa would be tons more fun if I did it with someone else. While climbing Mount Kilimanjaro is not a "technical" climb (no ropes or crampons needed), it is not easily summitted. Because of its height of 19,341 feet, you need to be very careful how quickly you ascend and to pay attention to a strict acclimatization schedule. When ascending via the standard Machame route, it takes five-and-a-half days to get to the summit, and one-and-a-half days to descend. Because tourism is the primary industry in Tanzania (climbing, safari), you are required to have porters to carry most of your gear and fix your meals while you slowly make your way to the top. Not a bad way to travel.

In my experience, if you want to build momentum for something that a lot of people would think "out there," it's a good idea to get support from people you're sure will give you the answer you want—yes. For me, that person is Caroline. If there's an adventure and it requires travel, 90 percent of the time, she'll be game. And hey, I'm doing it with my daughter. How many dads wouldn't love to strengthen their connection by spending a couple of weeks with their daughter on an epic adventure? Her response when I posed the idea to her was "You bet." We tentatively talked about climbing Mount Kilimanjaro in January or February of 2020. After we did some research, we learned there are two ideal times of the year when you can climb Mount Kilimanjaro and have a good chance of dry weather and beautiful skies at night.

The most popular time to climb Mount Kilimanjaro is during the summer when you're almost guaranteed a rain-free climb. The drawback is it's also a popular time so it can be crowded on summit day (crowded is relative, usually twenty-five or thirty people in the summer). The other time it's supposed to be dry is January and early February. The chance of large crowds after flying halfway around the world for an epic experience didn't thrill me, so Caroline and I decided the winter window looked attractive. We would climb the tallest peak in Africa—one of the seven summits—in January when there would be less people and great weather. This would be perfect! Now, it was just a matter of checking to see if we could get a team of friends together so we could do a private climb and control the dates, instead of going on a regularly scheduled climb.

Since a few people I knew had shown interest in climbing Mount Kilimanjaro over the years, I sent a blanket email out to Joe Matheson, Drew Chrisohon, Reggie Blackburn, Pete Shepard, and Jim Zingerman. The climb eventually also included Doug Corbett and Mai Herr—making the group nine in total, including myself and Caroline.

Once I sent the initial email, I expected a few people to be busy and unable to commit. Although somewhat surprised, the response was phenomenal. Joe Matheson (son of my buddy who died in the climbing accident) was one of the first to confirm he would go. He had gotten into mountaineering soon after I got Pete hooked on the pastime. Joe was a couple of years younger than Caroline. He had been a cross-country runner in high school and had become a respected triathlete over the years, both in and post college, even traveling as far as Finland based on his qualifying times. He had the endurance to do something like this and was also up for challenges.

Joe had joined in on one of the Mount Adams climbs we did with Foursquare Mountaineering when my son and Pete did it together. He also climbed to the summit of Mount Whitney (14,508 feet/4,402 meters), the highest peak in the contiguous United States, with Caroline and I just after his dad had died. Not only was Joe very capable of summitting, but the connection between our families from losing someone we loved and respected would add to the trip's power.

From there, I went with people closer to my age. Pete Shepard was still doing some climbing and extensive hikes even after we both left Tree Top in the Yakima Valley. Having the person along who got me into climbing would make the trip special. I dropped him a note. "Yup, I'm in" was his response. In addition to Pete, it would be great to have another member of the Foursquare club coming with us. Jim Zingerman was all in when I mentioned going to

Mount Kilimanjaro. He had zero hesitation, and I was thrilled he said yes. As mentioned before, Jim is a great person to have along on these types of adventures. First, he's a physician. While we've never put that pressure or title on him when we went on adventures or climbs, it never hurts to have someone with a medical background instead of the rest of us who would most likely wing it if we got into a medical situation based on our basic first aid skills. In addition to being a physician, Jim can be the calm and logical person you need on adventures since something out of the ordinary always seems to happen that requires great thought.

Drew Chrisohon and I worked together at Golden State Foods (my employer at the time). I had mentioned to Drew that I might want to climb Mount Kilimanjaro someday. His response was always, "Let me know if it gets serious." Drew was born and raised in the South, and his Southern charm and humor makes him a great guy to be around. He's laid back, but cranial, and he has such varied interests that I started calling him the "Renaissance man." Drew is also an eagle scout and was heavily involved in Boy Scouts after graduating from college. Based on that and his being an avid fisherman and hunter, I knew an outdoor adventure would be right up his alley. He was also turning forty that year and wanted to do something monumental for his birthday.

Everyone was my close friend or family member, as well as someone I could see as a great climbing partner. We could spend more than a week together without getting on each other's nerves.

Mai Herr was a friend of Caroline's who became a family friend. When she came to visit us for the Fourth of July in 2019, we talked about the trip and the timing and invited her to come with us. She's a positive spirit with a smile that lights up a room. Only a week after getting home, she let Caroline know she would love to join us on the trip.

Reggie Blackburn and I knew each other from when we were on a tennis team together in Roswell, Georgia, before my family moved to Yakima in 2007. Soon after being on the tennis team, we found out we both had grown up in the Philadelphia area—me in the city and Reggie just outside Northeast Philadelphia in Lower Moreland. In fact, we both grew up on the same street but about half-a-dozen miles apart. The old degrees of separation theory really applied to Reggie and me. We became good friends from being on that team, but I never realized he was a big hiker until we came back to Atlanta for a wedding. One more baby boomer—what a great addition.

When I first mentioned climbing Kili to Reggie, he said he had a bunch of things going on so the timing might not be right. "No problem," I said. "Let me know if you change your mind." Soon after, he asked if there was still room. I said yes, but since it was in the late summer, I was concerned whether he was in good enough physical shape to take on the challenge. To this day, Reggie still gives me grief about questioning his physical condition.

A couple of months later in early fall, I mentioned climbing Mount Kilimanjaro to Doug Corbett, a fraternity brother and good friend, while he was over for dinner. I half-expected him to say no because he'd never climbed before. But you need to understand Doug—he's always been adventurous. Doug and I met at Penn State while belonging to the same fraternity, but he was a full year ahead of me. Just by chance, he was visiting for a weekend football game about a month before I graduated from college in the fall of 1981. He had moved to Hilton Head, South Carolina, and said if I needed a place to stay until I got a job, he was housesitting for a family on the beach. He mentioned he would be happy to help me find a job there, and I could live at his place for a while. I ended up taking him up on his offer, moving first to Hilton Head Island, South Carolina, and then Atlanta, Georgia.

Doug has never met a stranger—he's always outgoing and open to new experiences. His adventuresome spirit is reflected in how he ended up on Hilton Head after college. While driving home from Florida, he saw a sign for Hilton Head on I-95 and decided to take a break while driving back to Pennsylvania. Long story short, he met some people, became friends, and ended up living there for the next seven years.

When I mentioned to Doug about climbing Kili, he had never done any extensive hiking or climbed a mountain. But after talking about the climb in our kitchen, he soon said he wanted to join in. I stressed how difficult it would be and that he needed to train especially hard since he was joining the group late in the process, and I didn't want to let any of the other people down who had been training for the past half year. He assured me he would start a regular workout routine immediately, which he did.

So, that made nine people in total. What a mixed bag of friends and family—ranging in age from their late twenties to their mid-sixties! I had my daughter and a close friend, a few people from the climbing group in Yakima, a friend from Atlanta, and a buddy from college. They had never spent any time together for an extended period, but now they were going to tackle a difficult challenge together. Thinking back on it, had I thought about it further, I would have thought I was crazy. It's always amazing that the least planned get-togethers can turn out to be so magical, even when challenged in the most extreme situations.

We all decided to arrive in Arusha, Tanzania, on January 27, 2020. This arrival date would allow everyone to acclimate to the time zone changes and get rested up before we started climbing on January 29. Once everyone had met and grabbed dinner, I knew this would be a special time. The entire group melded together quickly, and I could tell our common goal of climbing this epic mountain would overcome any issues we might come across.

The day before our climb, we met our head guide, Raymond. He would be leading a group of porters, cooks, and guides in our pursuit of the summit scheduled to take place on February 4. Raymond was an unassuming, tall, and very thin Tanzanian who had a good track record on the mountain. When he spoke to us for the first time, I believe everyone was put at ease because of his soft-spoken, calm, and secure demeanor. He reviewed our itinerary and was very positive about our summit chances.

The day finally arrived! After almost a year of planning (let alone having this climb on my radar for a few years), we packed up our hiking and climbing gear on the morning of January 29 to climb the tallest peak in Africa. Expectations for all of us were very high. We had all trained hard and felt confident it was going to be a lifelong memory. I felt especially confident not only because of my training, but because I had an unplanned event around Joe's dad, Pete, being with us in spirit.

A memorial service had been held for Pete a few months after his accident. His wife, Donna, had asked me to come up with a playlist of Pete's favorite music, which I was thrilled to put together. When I woke the morning of January 29, I noticed the "Pete's Music" playlist was on my watch. It seemed too coincidental that this remembrance of Pete just happened to pop up when we were about to undertake such an extreme challenge. Both Joe and I took it as a message that he was going to be with us while we climbed.

At the main gate to start climbing Mount Kilimanjaro is a pack weigh station designed to regulate the weight the porters will carry. The scene there was like something out of an expedition movie. People and busses were everywhere! All shapes, sizes, and nationalities were in one small area, speaking a variety of languages and wearing a varying degree of climbing and hiking outfits. All this commotion just added to the excitement of the adventure and drove home that people from all over the world saw this as a big challenge to take on.

After the weigh-in, we all put our packs on. The porters loaded up all the extra gear we didn't carry on our backs, and we headed to the trailhead. After hiking about one-hundred yards of our forty-mile, 10,000-foot vertical climb, it started to rain. *Rain? But this is the dry season,* I thought. To climb the mountain, you go through five very distinct climate zones. You start in a rainforest and end up on a rocky, snow-covered peak after six days of climbing. While passing people, someone said what we were all thinking, "This is the rainforest portion." No worries; we would get through this mild rain and enjoy clear weather when we got to the dry arid section tonight and tomorrow.

Well, the light rain turned into a torrential downpour. While we had pack covers for our smaller packs, the porters with our remaining gear (tents, sleeping bags, and extra clothes) were carrying everything somewhat exposed to the elements. Despite the rains, we got to the first camp and were relieved to sit in a dry tent that was set up for us while our remaining gear was unloaded.

Then I realized the bag with my gear had been exposed to the pouring rain, and I had forgotten to line the large duffel with a trashcan liner. My gloves, sleeping bag, and extra clothes (supposed to be dry) were all damp or soaked. Ugh! This was not good since I knew wet items usually didn't dry very well on the trail, and we needed dry gloves and socks when summit day came around and the temps would plunge into the single digits or below. As we sat in the dining tent, I must admit my spirits weren't the best.

Here we were, halfway around the world, about to undertake an extreme challenge with varying weather conditions after training for almost a year, and most of my gear was sopping wet. The team picked up on my anxiousness and immediately started trying to pick up my spirits. After hearing about the situation, our lead guide, Raymond, immediately mentioned that they had an extra-dry sleeping bag and would help dry some socks and gloves over the cooking stove. Lesson learned. Don't freak out at the first sign of a problem. Try to remain calm, think it through, and gain the counsel of the people around you, and you will find a solution. While not ideal, we would be in good shape. It was the first of many hiccups we would encounter, but it was overcome with the help of the diverse group of people I was with who had a single goal.

Since you gain approximately 10,000 feet (3,048 meters) of altitude to climb this mountain, you need to be careful not to succumb to altitude sickness, which can set in if you try to gain too much altitude too quickly. Altitude sickness can range from a nauseous feeling in your stomach with a dull consistent headache to severe conditions called High Altitude Pulmonary Edema (HAPE) or High Altitude Cerebral Edima (HACE), which can be deadly if not dealt with properly. The strategy to avoid or minimize altitude sickness is to apply the Tanzanian guides' principle of hiking *pole pole* (Swahili for "slowly") while gaining altitude. The plan was to hike to a higher altitude during the day, then retreat to a lower altitude to sleep. You can also take the drug Diamox, which requires a prescription; it aids by metabolizing more oxygen in your system to prevent altitude sickness. We had all decided to take Diamox since it has few side effects and would dramatically increase our chances of summitting. It's commonly used for climbs above 10,000 feet.

Over the course of the next five days, we would hike distances varying from a few miles to thirteen miles for five to eight hours at a time, and we would gain an average of 3,000 to 4,000 vertical feet. The climb was steady and deliberate. Each day we would wake, grab a great breakfast prepared by one of the guides who served as a cook, take a lunch break, and then continue usually until early afternoon.

Over the next five days, however, it would continue to rain! Gentle rain, misting rain, hard rain—no matter what degree, it rained pretty much for the entire trip until we got to summit day. If you've ever had to hike in the rain for a few hours, it can really wear on you. You're never dry, and the pattering of rain on your rain jacket with the water running into your face can really be a mental drain. Most normal people would have gone crazy, started bitching about the rain, or become ornery and grumpy. Not this group of people—we had the goal to climb one of the highest peaks in the world! Being optimists, when the rain would start to lighten, we would all take off our rain jackets and pants and think, *It can't rain much more*, and enjoy a few hours of misting versus full-out rain.

At night, it rained so hard it was best to stay in your tents. The high point of the day was everyone meeting in the dining tent for meals. We would sit around a long table, talk, and generally get to know each other. Drew, in his textbook Southern manner, would tell stories in his strong accent about his days working at a chicken-processing facility and the guy who would walk through the chicken coops barefoot, exposed to the chicken dung. The stories brought tears to most of our eyes.

Multiple stories were told about families, past climbing experiences, times on the trail, and our homes. We played lots of music, including Toto's song "Africa," which references Kilimanjaro. Because we were at the beginning of the pandemic, we always went through a hand-washing routine using spray-on antibacterial spray and then a traditional hand-waving to get the spray to dry. Even with all the rain, the long days hiking, and continually hiking in wet boots, no one in our group ever got down on themselves or each other; rather, they did what you should do when less-than-desirable circumstances are thrown your way that you can't control—they dealt with it and remembered we were a team that was there to climb a mountain, and we were fortunate to have this opportunity not everyone has the chance to experience. Remarkable! We all remained in good spirits, and we even almost drew strength from the rain as a group because we were determined not to be deterred from our goal.

"Another glorious day, the air as delicious to the lungs as the nectar to the tongue."

— John Muir

All was looking good until we reached camp the day before we were scheduled to hike the steepest portion of the climb—the Barranco Wall, a class 4 rock scramble up an almost vertical face. That night, I could hear someone violently vomiting outside the tent. It was Pete Shepard. He had come down with a severe stomach virus and couldn't keep anything down. After Jim's evaluation and discussions with the guides, it was decided Pete would need to descend to avoid risking any further danger. To his credit, he did climb the challenging Barranco Wall while stopping to throw up along the way so he could get to a more direct path down to the bottom with one of the guides. We all felt horrible for Pete, but Pete was a realist. Once it was determined he couldn't go on, he simply accepted it and planned to head down. No "Woe is me" or getting mad, just "This happens, and I'm really thrilled to have gotten this far." A very commendable perspective.

After Pete left us, we continued in the rain until we reached our final camp the day before we would leave to climb to the summit early in the morning at an altitude of 16,000 feet (4,877 meters). After an early dinner, Raymond did our daily evening routine of measuring our blood oxygen level. This check is important since a low blood oxygen percentage is an indication of high chances of severe altitude sickness. We knew that if our level fell below 80 percent, we would be denied the chance to climb to the summit. Even though people joked and made light of this routine, it almost always made people a bit anxious. The last measurement before we went to bed in advance of our summit was not different. Everyone checked out well in the safe zone except for Jim and me. Our levels were on the edge. However, because of our experience climbing and hiking steady and strong during the previous days, it was decided we could continue with the team. Whew! I hadn't thought of there even being a small chance of that happening.

Summit day (better described as night) is an extremely anxious time. No matter which mountain you're climbing—Rainier, Adams, or Kilimanjaro—when you wake to climb to the summit (after a normal restless night's sleep), everyone is as excited as five-year-olds on Christmas morning. We were going to do this! It was about to really happen!

We started hiking out of high camp when, suddenly, our group came to a stop. Looking around, I could see Mai off to the side, and she looked like she was throwing up. Oh no! Altitude sickness. She tried to continue walking, but the sickness had come on hard; she was going to have to descend to be safe. Another heartbreaker. To be around Mai is to experience someone who is eternally optimistic and with a smile that will light up your day. To have had her come this far and be turned around on summit day seemed cruel.

In true fashion, though, once again no whining, no feeling sorry for herself; she simply resigned herself to the fact that her summit attempt was over. Raymond assigned one of the guides to climb down with her. We would meet up with her the following day at the lower camp just inside the park entrance.

Now we were down to seven on our summit attempt of Mount Kilimanjaro. Because your heart is pumping quickly from the excitement of summit day, you usually start out at a pace quicker than you should. The guides did a good job of slowing us down to a more deliberate pace, and soon we were on a steady ascent up the steep 3,400-foot vertical gain that would lead to the crater. There we would be able to stand on the top of Africa and pose at the famed wooden sign where lifelong memories would be recorded. It was a visual I had a hard time keeping out of my mind while staying focused on each step.

Summit day on Kilimanjaro is also like other climbs in that it's a long day. You go to bed early in the evening, wake up at around 11 p.m. after a restless night's sleep, then hike around six to seven hours up a steep incline to reach the summit to see the sunrise. After summiting and standing on the top for about thirty to forty minutes, you immediately start the six-to-seven-hour descent because staying at that high of an altitude for long can have detrimental effects. It's a twelve-to-fourteen-hour day that tests your mental and physical stamina; you're in a state of pain that makes you wonder why you ever wanted to do it in the first place—it's a strange affliction we climbers have. Excited with anticipation for summit day, elation at the top, then sometimes excruciating pain on the way down, swearing you will never do anything like this again—only to start planning the next great adventure a few weeks after returning, and telling everyone how phenomenal the experience was while forgetting all the pain you endured to get to the top.

After approximately five hours of grinding our way to the edge of the crater, we reached Stella Point at an altitude of 18,884 feet (5,756 meters). As the sun slowly began to rise, we rested for a minute and drank some hot drinks before plodding ahead toward the true summit, less than 516 feet higher. Even though that seems like a short distance, the combination of cold and altitude makes it difficult to breathe. The tendency is to try to go quicker, but the best way to summit is to maintain the *pole pole* strategy that had been drilled into us by our guides from the start. As we walked the final distance in single file with our guides, the sun was starting to peek above the horizon. It slightly brightened the snow, which made it glisten in the early morning light.

I was lined up behind Doug, who was walking fine; then, suddenly, he started wobbling, then fell over in the snow, catching himself on his knees. One of the guides and I picked him up by his jacket and steadied him. Then we all continued our walk in fresh, ankle-deep snow to the clearly visible summit sign, which marked the top of Mount Kilimanjaro—the tallest peak on the African continent.

After twelve months of planning, a nineteen-hour flight, six days hiking in the rain, and twenty-three miles hiking, gaining 14,051 feet (4,283 meters) of elevation, at 6:39 a.m. on February 3, 2020, we finally summited Mount Kilimanjaro! Once we arrived at the famous wooden sign, numerous shouts of joy and relief could be heard. Seven out of nine of our group had made it to the top, way above the average percentage. It was a truly remarkable scene!

Not only were we hugging and congratulating the people in our group, but we were all embracing the guides and porters who had worked so hard to help us get to the summit. At that point, no socioeconomic, national, racial, or religious differences existed among us. We were just a group of people who had suffered through six days of rain and now stood at the top of the tallest peak on the continent, enjoying a crystal-clear morning while the sun gradually brightened the day.

Suddenly, maybe because I saw Joe out of the corner of my eye, I started thinking about Pete Matheson and how great it would have been to have him along and how much I missed him. I also felt grateful to have this emotionally overwhelming experience with my daughter, who I had seen be born, grow up, and mature into a responsible and beautiful person. I was also thankful that Joe was there with Caroline. I considered how close our families are, and all that Joe had gone through in the past few years.

The three of us embraced while I bawled my eyes out and told them both how much I loved them. Someone in the background noticed us embracing and wished me a happy birthday. Little did I know my good buddy Reggie was there with his phone to capture the moment. Caroline, Joe, and I were in a massive bear hug, and he captured it in a single photo and live on video. I'll forever be grateful to him for his quick thinking to capture that moment!

Joe also spread some of Pete's ashes there—a tradition he had started years ago at the top of every peak he had climbed since Pete's death.

After what seemed like a billion pictures being taken, Raymond began pushing us to start our descent. He warned us we had stayed at the top longer than is healthy, so we needed to get going. While we had summitted, we still had a long trip ahead of us to get back to the base and out of any danger. As we started descending, the emotional high started to dissipate, and soon, we were plodding our way back down the mountain and toward the gate. Before that time, we needed to hike most of the way back to the level at which we had started. A five-day journey up would become a seven-hour journey down. When we got to our tents after an almost sixteen-hour day, nearly everyone staggered into their tents and fell asleep.

The following day, we woke, hiked another three to four hours, and were back at the trailhead. In two days, we had hiked down from a level of 19,400 feet to a level of 5,400 feet. The day before, we had reunited with Mai, who was waiting with that beaming smile and a hearty congratulations. After eating our first "normal" lunch in seven days and downing a few celebratory beers, we headed down for our final goodbyes to our guides and porters. Later that day, we would meet up with Pete Shepard at the hotel with another beaming smile, a hearty hug, and his sincere words of congratulations.

For the next three days after the climb, we went on safari—an experience unto itself. Finally, when we flew out of the airport in Arusha after the safari, we started to notice more than a few people wearing masks to cover their faces. This seemed a bit strange to us. Little did we know we would be the last group from Climb Kili (our expedition company) to climb Mount Kilimanjaro before COVID-19 set in and shut down the world.

WHAT I LEARNED

When we got home, the question was asked, "So, how was it?" Whew! How exactly do you answer a question like that after such an emotional and physical experience? My mind goes to the many levels of emotional and physical extremes this climb hit. We had traveled to Africa—a continent I had never dreamed of visiting—and gotten to see Tanzania, which is perceived as being on the poverty level, but with people who are so abundantly happy you're embarrassed about your preconceived notion. We got to spend a week with our guides and porters and witness some of the most hard-working people I've ever met who had smiles on their faces from the time we walked through the gate to start our trip until the time they waved and hugged us goodbye at the end.

We had endured six days of hiking in the rain, pushing ourselves to a physical extreme many in the group had never experienced before. The amazing part is the group not only survived the long hike slogging along in the rain to an altitude higher than anywhere in the US, but we thrived and embraced the rain as something that brought us all closer. Most of all, we had the chance to spend a week with people some of us had never met before the climb, and we became soulmates for that moment in time, like few people get to experience.

FIVE THOUGHTS ON PREPARING FOR THE UNEXPECTED

1. Prepare, plan, and then expect to be surprised.

2. Control what you can control; be flexible with what you can't.

3. Draw on others' emotions when you are hit with the unexpected.

4. Sometimes you're better off because of the unexpected.

5. Be humble.

SUMMARY

"Everything is created twice, first in the mind and then in reality."

— Robin S. Sharma

So, how was it? It was a blessing! It gave me a lesson on how to be humble, how to accept conditions you're handed, and how to find a way, with the help of others, not only to survive but to embrace and thrive when unexpected things are tossed your way. It also made me grateful for the friends I was now closer to, but also for the Tanzanian guides who had taught me so much about life.

At one point, Raymond asked me if we were all from the US. When I said, "Yes," he asked, "Do you have malaria in the US?" "No," I replied. "Do you have typhoid?" "No," I replied. "Do you have the sleeping sickness?" "No," I replied. At that point, he stated, "What a wonderful country you live in. You are so fortunate." That is true perspective and a reality check that will stick with me forever…and it was unexpected. That's how it was.

CHAPTER 7

BEING FLEXIBLE DUE TO WEATHER

"Getting to the top is optional, getting down is mandatory."

— Ed Viesturs

Going into a challenge lightly can quickly humble you. Have you ever seen or read about something and thought, *Hey, I could do that!?* Then, as you read further, you realize that accomplishing what you just read about involves a lot more than you thought. At that point, you think, *Huh...I didn't think of that.*

I had thought about climbing the Grand Teton in Wyoming ever since Joe Matheson had climbed it in August of 2018 as a hike-and-climb, car-to-car in one day. While it was described as a technical climb at the top (more than I had done before), that he hiked in, summitted, and returned to the car in one day made me start thinking it would be a good challenge. As I read more, it seemed very doable—if you knew how to manage the technical vertical steep climb at the end to the summit and then rappel down.

I learned many people summit The Grand, but they usually hike partway, camp overnight, then summit, and return the next day. At a height of 13,775 feet (4,199 meters), the Grand Teton is one of the more prominent peaks in Wyoming—second in height to Gannett Peak (13,810 feet/4,209 meters)— and is easily visible from Jackson and the surrounding area.

Legend says its name comes from French voyageurs who named it "*les Trois Tetons*" (The Three Breasts). A lesser-known version of how it was named states it comes from a Native American tribe, the Teton Sioux. I would imagine most people prefer the first version, especially if you've ever witnessed the Tetons' beauty. While argument exists over who was the first to summit the Grand Teton, Billy Owen and Rev. Franklin Spalding made an ascent of the Grand on August 11, 1898. Thus, the name of the main hiking route is the Owen-Spalding route, largely based on some extreme self-promoting by Billy Owen. Climbing the Grand Teton via the Owen-Spalding route involves a 6.5-mile/5,000-foot gain hike to the Lower Saddle, and an additional 1.5-mile/2,000-foot vertical gain to get to the top.

After Mark McGuire (Foursquare Mountaineering) moved to Bozeman, Montana, from Yakima and I moved to Atlanta, Jim Zingerman (who still lived in Yakima), Mark, and I started meeting up in the winter to ski at the Big Sky Resort outside of Bozeman. Mark's son, Nicholas, would often join us, help to bring the average age down, and demonstrate how to jump, bounce, and ski backward down the mountain. Mark and his son are the two most impressive skiers I know.

During one of those trips, we discussed climbing the Grand Teton. Since we had all hiked and climbed together, we felt good about the chemistry and our ability. The only aspect different from previous climbs was the very technical part at the top. Since Mark and Nicholas are also excellent technical rock climbers, we felt good about being able to handle the vertical part at the top. Once Caroline decided to get married in June near Park City, Utah, it seemed natural to incorporate a climb up The Grand in Wyoming—a short driving distance from Salt Lake City. We decided we would set June 28-30 to be the dates to climb.

Although the climb is easily accomplished in two days (when sleeping at the Lower Saddle), we thought it would be wise to build in an extra day in case we encountered bad weather. During the winter of 2022, we secured camping passes for two nights. That way, we would have extra time budgeted to camp and allow Mark and Nicholas to climb additional peaks if we accomplished the Grand summit in two days. Good plan!

After training in Atlanta that winter and spring at the usual spots that included Kennesaw Mountain and Stone Mountain, the trip finally arrived. The wedding went off without a hitch. I dropped Mary off at the airport and said our goodbyes (including not to contact Caroline if something bad happened). Then I drove to Driggs, Idaho, to meet up with Jim at the home of our friends, Ned and Kathryn Rawn. We had stayed with Ned and Kathryn during the winter seasons when we would make our way down from Bozeman to ski with Ned at Grand Targhee and Jackson Hole.

The Rawns are always great hosts, and Kathryn is a phenomenal cook. After a heavy carb dinner, Jim and I went to bed with plans to get up early and head to the Ranger station at Jenny Lake in the Grand Teton National Park where we would pick up our camping passes. Mark and Nicholas drove down to the Jenny Lake parking lot. They would be camping in the park that night and meet us at the ranger station. Before going to bed, Jim and I looked at the weather. That night, we went to bed with the observation that the weather looked phenomenal! The hike would start out warm, then cool off as we got higher. Winds didn't look too bad. Some snow was reported as you got higher, but it didn't look like we would need crampons for the hike. Things were looking perfect.

On June 28, we woke up in Driggs to a beautiful day. Cool temps, low winds—perfect for hiking. After breakfast, we headed out to the ranger station in the park where we would pick up passes, meet up with Mark and Nicholas, and head to the trailhead to start our climb. During the drive from Driggs to Jackson, Jim and I could clearly see the goal we had come to accomplish. The Grand Teton was standing out in the morning light, just calling us to climb it.

When we passed Jackson Hole with the Grand Teton in full sight, looking like you could reach out and touch it, I decided to put on Eminem's "Lose Yourself" to get us pumped up. We would be hiking to the Lower Saddle via the Garnett Canyon trail—the usual route that's used. Soon, we were at Lupine Meadows' parking lot and trailhead after picking up our passes and packing up for the hike. Mark and Nicholas were carrying most of the technical climbing gear. Nicholas was carrying more than his fair share of weight…of course. When we packed up, I decided to leave my wallet in Jim's car so it would be secure, and I only packed my driver's license in my pack.

We started out with all the usual friendly banter and excitement that happens at the start of any of these adventures. Soon, we were on the trail hiking along in the woods on our way to the Lower Saddle. There we would set up camp in preparation for a summit attempt the following morning. The day continued to be phenomenal. On the hike up, as the trees gradually thinned, we gained altitude, then passed a few streams and meadows blooming with bright yellow flowers.

In the distance when we reached a clearing, we could see down into the valley below. Just before leaving the wooded part of the hike, we ran into a park ranger who asked for our camping pass. Huh, I had never had a ranger ask for any type of documentation before, let alone ask to physically see it when we said we had the proper credentials. "Doing his job, I guess." (But are they only there to hassle us?) Soon, we reached the rock and boulder scramble at around 9,500 feet that I had read about on the All-Trails app. At that point, the trail became less defined as we scrambled and plodded our way along, trying to stay on the trail, which was the most direct way to the Lower Saddle.

About five miles into our 6.5-mile hike, the temps got a little cooler so Mark and Nicholas changed from shorts into longer hiking pants. I thought that was the sign of true pros. Jim and I wore long pants and were a little warm at the start; Mark and Nicholas started out in shorts, were probably more comfortable, and then changed clothes when things got cooler. Their experience was shining through.

After another little while, we reached the steep part of the trail that would put us at the Lower Saddle. We decided to hike up through a narrow snow-covered chute between two towering rock formations instead of the direct route up the vertical wall using the fixed rope that's there. Fortunately, we had all decided to pack our crampons, so we donned them, grabbed our ice axes at the end of the trail, and walked horizontally across a small snowfield and then up the steep narrow pitch. Most of the way up the chute, you can veer left and scramble over a boulder field that leads to the top of the chute, then hike to the various rock-protected camping spots at the Saddle.

By that time, it was late afternoon, so we unpacked our tents and camping gear, chose a place to pitch our tents, and got all set for dinner and our night camping at the Saddle in anticipation of pushing for the summit in the morning of June 29. Morale was high, although it was a bit breezy while we were setting up our tents. No problem; that was to be expected. We were thinking we would get up in the morning, have a casual breakfast, and climb the Grand Teton. The plan was to summit tomorrow, then come back to camp and decide whether we wanted to camp another night or head back down to the cars. All was good; everything was on schedule.

But Mother Nature had a different plan. During the night, the winds started to increase at the Saddle. When we woke the next day, the winds were blowing harder—nothing unbearable—but enough to give us pause. In the morning, Mark and Nicholas also checked the weather. They noticed a chance of thunderstorms in the area. You might consider pushing through a lot of conditions to summit a mountain—rain, snow, wind—but the chance of lightning while fully exposed on top of a 12,000-foot peak made the decision not to climb a no-brainer. We were making a wise decision—something we're not always known for. Experience was coming into play. We spent most of the day resting, eating, and exploring the Lower Saddle. Such delays are routine when climbing since a summit is usually weather-dependent, and weather is something you cannot precisely predict.

While we were hanging out at the Lower Saddle, the winds gradually increased to the point where we needed to secure and resecure our tents. When exploring the other side of the Saddle, I noticed the campsite and tents of one of the guide companies. They had heavy North Face tents that looked permanently secured into the ground. That seemed like slight overkill to me, but I guess they took precautions because the tents would be there the entire climbing season.

The wind continued to increase. Toward the end of the afternoon, you could barely stand when walking from tent to tent. Mark and Nicholas still seemed positive about our summit chances since the winds were forecasted to decrease during the night. While at dinner, as the winds howled even stronger, Jim decided he would not be heading for the summit in the morning because of the weather. No problem; we always respect individual decisions. At that time, we also discussed the plan for the next day. Mark and Nicholas had packed and carried up two climbing ropes to make certain we had enough equipment for four of us to summit. Since only three people at most would climb the technical part the next day, Mark asked if he could leave the 10.5-mm/60-meter (100-foot) climbing rope at camp, and if one of us could carry it down to lighten their load on the way down after summiting. The rope was almost eight extra pounds of dead weight.

Jim, being the nicer guy, volunteered to carry the rope. While he volunteered, I have to say my selfishness came into play that day. Instead of getting "alligator arms" that come with not wanting to pick up a dinner check, I became the mime Marcel Marceau and didn't speak when he asked who should carry it. Like I've said, Jim is a great guy!

Because the winds increased again before we went to bed, I spoke with Mark and decided if the winds maintained or increased, I would probably not go in the morning either, but I would make that call in the morning. We went to bed that night agreeing we would head out around 4 a.m. for our summit attempt. If I decided not to go, Mark and Nicholas would text us about how they were coming along and whether we should wait for them or head back to the trailhead, head back to Driggs, and meet up with them at Ned and Kathryn's house. I hoped to join them in the morning, but I had started to doubt that would be the wise choice.

What a wild night it became! Instead of the winds decreasing, they continued to increase. Later, we learned the wind speed was steady at 40 mph with a gust up to 50 mph. That was not conducive to a good night's sleep before one of the most technical climbs of my climbing career. I found out that night how much wind my small, REI Quarter Dome SL1 tent could withstand. All night, I could hear the steady winds pound the tent's outside, and any loose flap became uncontrollable in the raging wind.

The night was quite the experience. As I lay in the tent listening, the wind would occasionally decrease to a dull roar. The first time it happened, I thought, *Great. The winds are dying down; the summit is a real possibility.* Once the wind reached a normal level, I heard what sounded like a freight train coming my way. Shortly after, I realized the winds were picking up again to their peak from the other side of the Saddle; they made their way to my slightly exposed tent and started pounding the tent again with a vengeance.

> *"Between every two pines is a doorway to the new world."*
>
> *— John Muir*

At various times, the severe wind caused some of the tent stake lines to become loose and start snapping. I had to get on my hands and knees in the middle of the pitch-black night to repair them by retying the two broken pieces together in one knot. At the same time, I would add extra rocks to the side of the tent and the tent stakes to prevent the tent from coming loose and blowing away or simply exploding into pieces of torn cloth. As severe gusts became steadier, the sides of my tent started to bow to the point that, at the top, they almost touched. At the base of the tent, where I was sleeping, the tent bowed in so much that two sides were pinched together with my sleeping bag as the only thing keeping them from meeting. I worried the tent poles would break under the fifty-plus mph winds, causing the tent to explode and forcing me to scramble down to where Jim, Mark, and Nicholas had pitched their tents. At that point, I sat up and pressed my back against the tent's windward side in hopes of pushing back against it so the tent wouldn't explode. While it was good to save the tent, it was impossible to get any sleep.

While I sat pushing against the tent's windy side, the gust would increase so much it would push me until I was almost bent over at a forty-five-degree angle inside the tent. All night long, I kept looking at my watch to determine how much longer it would be until 4 a.m. when Mark and Nicholas might be headed out to push for the summit. At about 3 a.m., I was finally able to lie down and fall asleep. A short time later, I heard people outside my tent and then Mark's voice asking if I was coming along. "Don't think so," I said. "Good luck." After a night with almost no sleep and hearing the winds still blowing hard, I decided not to go with them. Not only was I not very rested and concerned for myself, but I didn't want to be a liability to them and risk none of us succeeding if they had to turn around because of me. I was comfortable with the decision. However, it did bring back bad memories of being with Mark on Mount Baker.

During the hike up Mount Baker, after skinning up to a camping spot in the snow the previous day, I had told Mark to go to the top without me. I had felt spent and not up for the skin up/ski down from the summit. Those are the only two times I made the call not to summit after getting close to the top. It's a personal decision each climber must make, no matter how high the mountain you're attempting to conquer. Nor does the decision come easily. Most climbs usually require months of preparation, including conditioning, buying the right equipment, and thinking constantly about the challenge you're about to undertake.

After Mark and Nicholas headed out, I went back to sleep for a few hours. I was comfortable with my decision, but disappointed this wasn't my day. When I woke, I walked down to where we had been eating our meals and saw Jim sitting there and eating breakfast. We chuckled about the severe conditions the night before. Jim told me he hadn't slept much either, and he was amazed our tents had survived one of the windiest nights we had experienced after ten years of climbing various high peaks. We took that time to commend ourselves on our wise decision. "Guess we're getting smarter in our old age," said Jim.

We then discussed whether we were getting too far along for these types of adventures; maybe we should stick with skiing and day hikes. Jim and I had been through some great adventures together over the years, including Dragon Tail Peak, Mount Baker, Three Finger Lookout, and our mind-blowing summit of Mount Kilimanjaro. Maybe it was time to slightly dial it back. Jim was confident about his decision; I was on the fence.

While packing, we noticed the climbing rope Mark and Nicholas had left for us to carry down. As we started to pack, a park ranger walked by our campsite on his way to the summit of the Grand. "How's it going, guys?" he asked. Recalling our previous meeting with a ranger, I noticed he was wearing a National Parks visor. I'd never seen them wear one; they usually wear the nylon and mesh baseball caps. *Quite an improvement,* I thought.

We told him we were doing well, the story of our night at the Saddle, and that the other two members of our group had headed toward the summit earlier in the morning. We also told him we would be heading down shortly since we had gotten a text from Mark that they were delayed on the way up and we should head down. "Planning on glissading?" he asked. "Yes, we are," we replied, internally rolling our eyes. "Make sure," he said, "you can see where you're going, and be certain to control your speed." Again, we did an internal eye roll.

Glissading is like sledding on your butt. It makes descending much easier since you can cover ground a lot quicker while sitting up with your feet facing down and sliding instead of the sometimes-painful hike down—and it's a lot more fun! The standard procedure of glissading entails holding your ice ax to one side with the handle part (spike at the end of the shaft) in the snow to work as a rudder and to control your speed. Mountain climbers also use an ice ax to "self-arrest" if they feel they are going too fast or if they fall and start to slide high on top of a glacier. If you fall or must stop while glissading, you simply roll over onto your stomach and dig the ice ax into the snow (the pick on the head) as hard as you can. Then you slam your toes into the ice to stop your descent. It's practiced often in advance of a big mountain climb.

We considered ourselves experienced climbers, not first-timers who didn't know how to glissade. "Will do," we responded politely. Once the ranger left, we finished breakfast, packed our gear and what was left of our tents, and got ready to head down.

A lot of people pray the "I promise, and I'll never…" prayer when they feel they are in life-or-death situations. "I promise I'll be a better person. I promise I'll be nicer to my wife. I promise I'll give more to charities. I promise I will never do this again." While I'm not in the habit of praying that way, I did throw an

"I promise…" prayer out there during that long sleepless night because of the extreme conditions and because I wondered how we would get out of there if the conditions didn't change. "If you get me out of here safely," I prayed, "I promise I'll be a better person and make certain to do more homework before tackling something like this again." Little did I know I shouldn't have wasted my "I promise" prayer on that incident.

WHAT I LEARNED

Sound decisions like hiking down make you feel good inside after the disappointment and regret pass. While my wife has sometimes wondered about my decision to climb mountains, I've always assured her we usually make smart decisions and do not have a death wish. Since the Tetons—especially the Grand Teton—is estimated to be more than 10,000 years old, I knew it would still be there if I wanted to go back to climb it another day.

Living through that sleepless night also made me realize I should never take a climb for granted. Everything I read about it said it was very doable. Amputees, people who can't see, six-year-olds, and eighty-year-olds have all summitted the Grand. Joe Matheson did it in a day without an issue. We planned to do it in two to be more conservative and have more fun. The sleepless night also shook me a bit. The conditions were so extreme I was concerned whether we would make it down or whether my tent would explode, exposing me to the elements and all the unknown things involved with that.

FIVE THOUGHTS ON BEING FLEXIBLE DUE TO WEATHER

1. Weather forecasts are estimates, not statements of guaranteed facts.

2. Be prepared for changing circumstances.

3. Mother Nature is impersonal.

4. When weather changes your plans, accept it and move on.

5. Start thinking about an alternate plan when weather changes.

SUMMARY

"Life is 10% what happens to us and 90% how we react to it."

— Charles R. Swindoll

We had planned a schedule based on good conditions. Then the conditions changed dramatically. Even though we had scheduled extra time, Mother Nature had other plans. Deciding to take a pass, after a sleepless night, was the best route forward for Jim and me. Mark and Nicholas felt comfortable moving forward and going for the summit. We were comfortable with our decision; they were comfortable with theirs.

CHAPTER 8

LISTENING TO THE EXPERTS

"The future depends on what you do today."

— Mahatma Gandhi

Sometimes, it's good just to be on cruise control. Have you ever been working or doing something so involved that you thought, *I would just like to cruise along for a while*? When hiking, and especially when mountaineering, you get to the point where you think, *This is a cakewalk. Let's just cruise down the trail and get back to the car. I'm kind of spent and just want to enjoy the day, not focus on putting one foot in front of the other or trying to find a route.*

That was our mindset as we packed up at the Lower Saddle on June 30, 2022. We had spent the first day pushing to get to the Lower Saddle. We spent the next day wondering if we would get the chance to attack the summit. After that, we spent a sleepless night wondering if our tents would explode from the 40 mph winds and be blown down into the valley below. We were happy with our decision to hike down. We just wanted to enjoy the hike, take in the beautiful surroundings of the Grand Teton National Park, and get out of the wind that constantly rang in our ears like an oncoming train that never arrives.

Once we packed, including the rope Jim had so graciously agreed to carry, we started down. Before leaving, Jim donned his crampons since we would be down-climbing a steep chute just to the climbers' left of the Lower Saddle headwall. From there, we could reach the trail so we could descend to our car. Because crampons are like a series of sharp ice picks that strap onto the bottom of your boot, I decided to hike in my boots. I thought I could put my crampons on once we got to the steep chute; that way I could avoid walking across the boulder ridge and potentially slipping.

Once we got to the top of the steep chute, I realized I'd forgotten exactly how steep it was. (Looking down a steep chute is a completely different feeling from looking up at it). Now this approximately 150-foot long, 20-foot wide, 45-50-degree alley covered in snow immediately got my attention. While I put my crampons on at the edge of the rock ridge running parallel to the chute, Jim started the slow process of down-climbing toward a landing that would lead us to flat ground and then a short walk to the trailhead.

Down-climbing can be a bit intimidating, especially when coming down a steep hill. While you feel more in control facing the hill in front of you than facing the hill and back-pedaling, the descent's angle always seems more severe to me. This downclimb reminded me of our descent from the summit of Mount Hood years ago. While that one was significantly longer and more severe, possibly ending in you sliding thousands of feet into a sulfur pit (severely injuring yourself or even dying), I had the same thought process now. *Take your time. Keep your stride wide enough so your crampons don't catch the inside of your pants, and whatever you do, don't fall.* A fall within this chute, while not ending in a sulfur pit, would still have you sliding about a thousand feet onto the snowfield below. With crampons on, you stood the chance of breaking your leg or ankle if they caught before you had the chance to self-arrest with your ice ax.

Jim started his climb down in a diagonal direction, tacking his way back and forth in efforts to reduce the steepness. We planned for him to go halfway down to a rock landing in the middle of the snowy chute and stay there while I started my descent. That way, if I started to fall, he could get out of the way. Also, if he started to fall, I would be above him and could aid him. Good plan! As I methodically started down toward the rocky area Jim was on, he watched. Once I reached Jim, he started down again. He made his way to the chute's bottom and started hiking diagonally across its base toward the trailhead that started in the boulder field to our left.

Slowly and deliberately, I made my way to the bottom, which opened to a wide snowfield. Then I followed the path Jim had taken directly to the left on a worn trail in the snow. It led me to Jim on the boulder field. Once there, we were amazed the wind had almost completely stopped because it was being blocked by the headwall behind us. Without wind, the temperature increased significantly. Now, instead of clear skies and roaring winds, we had clear skies and a bright shining day at least fifteen degrees warmer than when we had left camp. We looked around and took time to enjoy the day. Standing on the rock field, we looked down on the large snowfield to our right and the Teton Valley in the distance below. This was why we climb!

When we got to the boulder field, which would start our descent guided by a visible trail on solid ground, we sat down, took off our crampons, shed some of our outer layers to cool off, and packed everything, including our ice axes, into our packs. "We won't need these again," we said to ourselves. We also grabbed our hiking poles, which had been lashed on the sides of our packs, and started the walk down to the tree level and then back to the car. *This is going to be a cruise,* I thought. *We've gotten through the most difficult part and can now enjoy a beautiful day while hiking down.* While we were still above the trees at around 11,000 feet, it would be smooth sailing from here.

As we hiked the rocky trail, we looked at the large, expansive snowfield to our right. "We should be glissading," I said to Jim. We had discussed glissading at the Lower Saddle while we were packing. Since we had already packed our ice axes into our packs, we felt we could glissade by putting both of our shortened hiking poles in our hands and putting them to the side—which would be similar to using an ice ax. Between the poles, our feet, and the snow being soft from the heat, we thought we would be in good shape and safe. It was a beautiful day with calm winds and warm temps. A fun slide in the snow would cool us down and be a kick.

We walked diagonally out to the middle of the snowfield, shortened our poles, made sure everything was secure in our packs, and discussed our route. When we looked at the snowfield from this new position, we realized we could go one of two paths. I looked at the trail path on my All-Trails app. (I had downloaded the route a couple of days before.) While the path to the right side of a rock ridge divider seemed more direct to get us on the path below the snow and in the trees, we couldn't see past what looked like a ridge about halfway down. Taking the ranger's advice to heart, we decided to glissade down the snowfield to the left of the rocks, then stop on what looked like a flat landing; we would assess next steps from there.

Jim took off first, slowly sliding with poles in hand, and made his way to the flat area we had identified. When he stopped, he gave the go ahead sign that it was safe for me to proceed down the snowfield to where he was standing. When I started sliding, I again thought about how beautiful the day was and how fortunate I was to be in the outdoors this way with my good friend. When I reached Jim and stopped, we both had huge smiles on our faces. We laughed and were giddy with happiness about the day. Once again, we looked down the next snowfield and planned our route and where to stop. Although this snowfield looked slightly steeper, we both felt confident we could control our speed based on the previous glissade. We identified another rock outcropping below us and agreed Jim would glissade to that spot, give me the go ahead, and we would meet there. *Same plan, same result,* we thought. *No problem.* This was getting to be fun and much better than the laborious hike down the trail farther to our left and above us.

Jim started sliding down. He seemed to be going at a good speed, with snow spraying up as he dug his boots in to control his speed. Once he came to a stop, he was saying something to me, but because I was some distance above him, I couldn't hear what he said and just assumed it was, "All good. Come on down." However, that's not what he was saying. Jim had realized the pitch of this snowfield was significantly steeper than the previous one. Since snow is all white, it's hard to correctly estimate the angle of the descent when you're on a snowfield.

Jim also realized that just before he reached the rock outcropping, he was slightly out of control. Once he got there, he discovered a cliff that dropped down just past where he was standing. From his vantage point, the drop-off went into a hole in the snow next to the Spalding Falls.

While Spalding Falls is completely exposed during the warmer months after all the snow and ice has melted, during the winter, spring, and early summer, it's covered by ice and snow. Because of the fall's torrential straight drop down, however, the water continues to flow freely under the snow. Plus, the raging water and spray that accompanies it will form an ice moat—an eroded path running parallel to it under the snow. Ice moats are one of the dangers of hiking on glaciers and snow-covered trails. Sometimes while hiking in the winter and spring, you hike up to what looks like a small hole in the snow; then, when you get closer, you can see a wide-open expanse under the snow and hear the raging water flowing hundreds of feet below. Jim had often confided to us that one of his fears was falling below the snow into an underground stream and drowning.

Jim was shouting to let me know about the cliff and waterfall as I started my descent on what seemed like a harmless glissade. Halfway into my glissade, I picked up speed and had a hard time slowing down, using the combination of my hiking poles and feet, to dig into the snow unlike an ice ax would have done. At one point, I was leaning on my poles on my right side with such pressure that they were bowed to the point of breaking. I was heading toward Jim at an accelerated rate of speed and would have a hard time stopping where he was standing.

Since he stood on a rocky outcropping next to a large boulder, I thought, *It's really going to hurt when I hit those rocks.* Well, that didn't happen. Instead of hitting the rocks and bounding off a car-size boulder to come to a stop, I accelerated toward the cliff and a two-and-a-half foot opening in the snow. In a split second, I flew past Jim, thinking if I timed it right, I could leap over the hole and onto the snow on the other side—even though the hole was a significant drop from where I would leave the ground. It's amazing how things slow down in moments of terror.

When I saw the opening, I thought about balling up my legs underneath me and then pushing off the ground at the last minute in hopes of "Supermaning" over the opening in the snow. That didn't happen. Instead, when I went to leap, I slammed into the other side, hitting my hands and my chest.

Although things then got foggy, I do remember a few items very clearly. First, I remember slamming into the far side of the opening and feeling like the wind had been knocked out of me. I then remember floating, like when you fall in a dream and are unsure when it will end. My guess is that once I hit the other side of the opening, I was knocked unconscious, either because of the impact or an involuntary bodily reaction. That's the last thing I remember until I became conscious on a ledge in the ice moat with the roar of the waterfall to my right, a steep vertical cliff in front of me, and ice walls behind me and to my left. When I looked down, I saw I had landed on a three-foot-wide ledge and was standing upright. My two pinky fingers hurt like they had been dragged along an asphalt road, and I was completely soaked with thirty-three-degree glacial water spraying me.

When I looked up, I could see a thin slice of sunlight fifty to sixty feet above and between one and two feet wide. Other than that, it was pitch black because I was so deep under the snow. It was also very loud because of the raging Spalding Falls to my right. I was soaking wet and starting to shiver from being cold. I could barely see my hands and feet in front of me. When I looked down, I saw I was standing on an ice ledge approximately three feet wide.

My subconscious was working overtime from all the extreme sounds and sensory overload. The ledge I stood on connected the solid rock wall to the solid ice wall behind me. As I looked down, I saw the Seattle Kraken hockey team hat my son had given me for my birthday. I thought about grabbing it since it had special meaning, but I feared any extreme movements might cause the ledge to break away, sending me down farther into the dark, wet abyss. At least I didn't feel any pain, except a small pain in my lower back, and my left hip hurt a little.

Then I heard a subconscious voice say, "Stay calm. Breathe slowly." I knew if I panicked, it would be a very bad thing. While trying to slow my breathing, I heard a soft prophetic voice whisper, "This is not your day to die." Realizing if I was going to get out, I would need my hands, I started blowing on them one at a time and sticking them in my mouth to warm them up. It helped a little, but they still hurt on one side (probably from slamming into the opening when I entered the hole).

After fifteen minutes, I began thinking about how I would get out of there. Realizing Jim had seen me slide into the hole, I called his name in a loud, panicky voice. I shouted so loud my voice hit a higher pitch and sounded like a boy's voice changing during puberty. I called Jim's name a couple of more times, but I didn't hear any response. I knew it would be difficult for him to hear me because of the loud waterfall. I started looking around to figure out how I would get out, even though I didn't see a clear option.

Up above, Jim was dealing with his own panicking. When he saw me glissading toward him out of control, he tried to think of how to slow me down, knowing what was on the other side of him. To his credit, he decided not to jump on top of me; if he had, we would have ended up in the ice moat together without anyone knowing where we were. The last thing Jim saw was me sliding past him at a high speed, then me shouting "Oh shit!" as I went into the hole and disappeared. Then there was silence.

Jim didn't hear me hit anything or any more screaming. Just silence. His immediate thought was, *Life is about to change. I just saw my buddy die.* He later mentioned he felt helpless, not knowing what he could do.

After a short time, Jim heard me calling his name from inside the hole. Then he tried calling 911, but he didn't have cell phone coverage. Now, he had a completely different desperate feeling: *My buddy didn't die during the fall.*

However, because he is a physician, he knew I only had a short time before hypothermia would set in from being under the snow. His thought now was, *My buddy is alive, but now I'm going to have to listen to him calling my name while he dies a slow death from hypothermia.*

Then Jim screamed out a prayer in the canyon. "Lord, I need your help… now!" Prayer is something many people do on a regular basis with the hope God will give an answer sometime in the future. Ironically, Jim had shared a story of his grandson losing his fishing pole and praying, "God help me find my pole." He was with Jim at the time and turned to him and said "Opi (what Jim's grandson calls him), when will God answer my prayer?" Jim, seeing this as a life-teaching moment, told his grandson God answers prayers in his time since there is a master plan. When Jim sent his prayer for help that day, he demanded an answer "now!" so there wouldn't be any confusion about the immediacy of the need. After a couple of seconds, the word "rope" came to him. "That's right; I agreed to carry the rope, and it's in my backpack!"

"Wilderness is not a luxury but a necessity of the human spirit."

— John Muir

Down below, I searched frantically for some handholds on the wet, slippery, flat rock face in front of me. I'm not a regular rock climber, but I had taken an REI rock-climbing class in preparation for this climb and knew even the smallest crag or sharp peak would be enough to grab onto and climb out.

Up above, Jim had gotten the hundred-foot rope and started throwing it into the hole where he thought I had gone in. Unfortunately, the backwash caused by the raging waterfall kept pushing the rope back up. Finally, Jim started leading it down into the hole—like when you fish and slowly let out the line. Now, it was at least going down into the hole at a regular pace.

After looking at the sheer wet face of rock in front of me and the cold, dark environment, I started wondering if the voice inside my head was wrong and these might be the final moments of my life. While I continued to look for a rock or a way to climb out and I kept trying to breathe slowly, it didn't look like any way out existed. I thought about my daughter's wedding the week before and how great an event it had been. I also thought about my conversation with Mary when she dropped me off at the airport, telling her not to call Caroline during her honeymoon if something happened to me. I called out to Jim a couple of more times, but my hopes were quickly evaporating of making it out of this situation alive.

About twenty-five minutes had now passed since I had landed on the ledge inside the ice moat. Studies say that exhaustion and unconsciousness from hypothermia start to happen in fifteen to thirty minutes; within thirty to ninety minutes, most people succumb to hypothermia and die a sleepy death. The time clock toward hypothermia was ticking.

Suddenly, I could feel a tapping on my right shoulder. Because it was dark down there, I wasn't sure what was hitting me on the shoulder. When I reached around with my left hand to blindly find out what was tapping me on the right shoulder and estimate where it was hitting me, I realized it was a rope! *A rope!* In that moment, everything changed. That rope was my lifeline and my first glimmer of hope. Just maybe I was going to survive. Just maybe I could climb up using the rope to escape a certain death.

At that moment, I was sure glad Jim had volunteered to carry the extra weight of the rope. Grabbing the rope, I tugged on it three times to let whoever was at its other end know I was there, alive, and ready to be pulled out. Surely, Jim had been able to reach the park rangers and a group of them were at the top, ready to pull me up.

After the three tugs, I pulled the rope down to get some extra length so I could wrap it around my waist and tie it in a knot. Before tying the rope around my waist, I unclipped the backpack that was still firmly on my back. I also wrapped the portion of the rope leading up to the opening around my left hand and then around my right—if for some reason the rope came off my waist, I would have a backup to keep from falling back in. I then wrapped the rope tightly around my waist and firmly knotted it. All I could think of was getting out, and now that I had a rope, I would do everything possible not to lose touch with it. I could feel someone on the other end pulling up the slack, but not with enough pressure to lift me out.

Drawing from my rock-climbing lessons, I leaned back, put my feet flat on the rock wall in front of me, and started walking up the wall, making certain to keep pressure on the rope. As I took small steps half the size of my foot, I realized someone was pulling up the slack. Hand-over-hand, one small footstep at a time, I started to scale the vertical wall in front of me in a reverse rappel. Slowly, I was making progress toward the small light opening above me. About halfway up, the ice wall behind me started to angle toward the rock wall in front. That allowed me to push my back against the ice wall while pressing with my legs on the rock wall.

Placing one foot at a time, I took slow, agonizing, and deliberate steps, one after another, while sliding my hands over each other as I gradually continued to make progress up the wall. After what seemed to be a very long time—as my arms burned, my legs shook, and my hands ached—I made it to the opening. When I popped out my head, I saw Jim sitting there alone with the rope wrapped around his waist, wedged into the steep rock slope, and crouching while pulling up the slack. Jim had an enormous smile on his face, and he was leaning back holding the rope taut. His huge Latvian calves were crouched under him, pressed against his chest to keep him from falling into the hole.

I had often commented to Jim that the reason he could hike so well was because of those calves…now I was grateful for them. Then Jim said something I'll never forget. "Dan, it's so good to see your face." Later, Jim would refer to this as a Lazarus moment—like Lazarus in the Bible, I had been raised from the dead. I still had another fifteen feet to go to reach Jim. "Don't let go!" I shouted in a half-panicked voice. "Of course, not," he said, mildly annoyed. I asked Jim to let me rest on the less-extreme part of the wall just below him for a few minutes. After a short rest, I pulled myself up to where Jim was crouched. "Where should I go?" I asked since the slope he was on was very steep, and I wasn't sure where it would be safe to lay down. "Jump on top of me," he said. So, I did. The two of us lay there in an embrace, laughing and crying at the same time. I was out!

Jim would say later that when he first saw my face, it was as white as a sheet, and when he touched my skin, it was cold as ice. He quickly wrapped his jacket around me. Then he tied the rope around my chest under my armpits. "I don't have any cell phone coverage," he said, "so, I'm going to tie you off and get a little higher to see if there's coverage up there." "Just don't let go," I said frantically, still paranoid of somehow slipping and falling back into the ice moat.

I could hear Jim scrambling up the rocky hill that felt like it was still at about a forty-three-degree angle. On his way up to tie off the rope, he also started blowing on the emergency whistle he carried specifically for an incident like this and yelling for help. Good thing Jim had read the wilderness survival book. After a few whistles, I could hear Jim talking to someone. I could barely hear the conversation. He identified himself as a park ranger and asked Jim what had happened. "My buddy is down there tied to the rope. He slid into a hole under the snow, and I thought he was dead," he told the ranger in an emotional voice.

Soon, the ranger made his way down to me, introduced himself as Noah Ronczkowski, and asked how I was doing. "Lots better" or something like it was my response. "What happened?" he asked. "I slid into a hole while glissading, fell fifty or sixty feet, and was under the snow for twenty-five minutes or so," I replied. Then I noticed the same National Park service insignia on his visor. Wow! "You're the same ranger we ran into up at the Lower Saddle earlier today!" "Yup," he said. Feeling a bit embarrassed and humbled, I told him I expected he would now give me a scolding about being careful while glissading. "Not at all," he replied. "No judgment here. I'm just glad you're alive."

WHAT I LEARNED

Advice is something you can choose to take or ignore. Sometimes, it ends up being the whisper you needed to make a wise decision. Other times, you ignore it and think, *I wish I had a do-over on that one.* Noah's advice to us about glissading—know where you're going and control your speed—might have helped us avoid the situation if we had chosen to follow it rather than thinking we knew it all.

I also learned the importance of having the correct equipment out and available so you can use it to properly do what you're trained to do in extreme circumstances. Not taking my ice ax out of my pack when we started glissading was a huge mistake that could have had horrible results.

FIVE THOUGHTS ABOUT LISTENING TO PEOPLE AND SURVIVAL

1. When someone with a voice of experience gently offers a suggestion, pay attention!
2. Double-check to make certain you're applying everything they said before proceeding.

3. When confronted with a life-or-death situation, try to remain calm.

4. Be prepared to have multiple options available when faced with a dire situation.

5. Never assume you know the answer for how you will survive.

SUMMARY

"Knowledge isn't power until it is applied."

— Dale Carnegie

Your parents give you advice, and sometimes you choose to take it; other times, you don't. Mine offered advice with great intentions. Because they raised us to be independent, I didn't always take their advice. Sometimes lessons are better learned when you experience the repercussions of those decisions—good or bad—firsthand.

There I was, lying on the side of a mountain, recovering from potential hypothermia, not sure what injuries were still unknown. The decision we made could have been fatal for me, Jim, or both of us. Yet here was Noah, the guy who gave us the advice and was now responsible for getting us down from 10,500 feet where we were isolated in a deep canyon. Rather than give me the scolding I deserved, he was gracious and consoling. Life happens, but so do miracles! I am eternally grateful to Jim Zingerman and Noah Ronczkowski for rescuing me off the side of the mountain that day.

CHAPTER 9

ACCEPTING CLIMBING'S INHERENT RISKS

"You, Lord, brought me up from the realm of the dead; you spared
me from going down to the pit. Sing the praises of the Lord, you
his faithful people; praise his holy name. For his anger lasts only a
moment, but his favor lasts a lifetime; weeping may stay for the night,
but rejoicing comes in the morning."

— David, Psalm 30:3-5

In the past, taking chances had tended to work out well for me. Taking
the chance to leave Philadelphia and head south after college ended
up being the perfect decision. It led to a fulfilling career that allowed
our family to do many things because of the pay. It led to meeting my
wife, who is the perfect person for me and someone I couldn't imagine
not going through life with. It led me to move to Yakima, Washington,
thereby dramatically changing my lifestyle. It led to me climbing
mountains and falling in love with the outdoors, which has led to a
much more fulfilling life than I could have imagined while growing up

in a major metropolitan area. Life comes with risk. I'm not talking about high risk—living on the edge and gliding in a wingsuit (wingsuiting or squirrel suit) down from the top of a mountain, but risk that expands your horizons and allows you to experience things you never thought possible. This time, unaware of how high the risk involved was, I had been lucky.

After Noah came down to me, he covered me with a sleeping bag he had in his pack. Then he started the process of assessing what injuries I might have. I was familiar with the process from having done some part-time guiding for REI and having to be wilderness first aid certified. Noah, however, had been EMT trained. During the assessment, I mentioned my left hip was starting to throb, my lower back was sore, and I had probably been knocked unconscious during the fall and had the wind knocked out of me. He also asked if I was on medications. I said I was on blood thinners. He then determined a helicopter rescue was in order, so he radioed to his lead to plan to lift me out of there. "They're tending to a fire right now, but I would expect them to be here in around forty-five minutes," he said comfortingly.

I was just glad to be out of that hole and starting to warm up. Noah was very good at keeping us calm. He asked us what we were doing and where we were from. When I shared I was out there for my daughter's wedding and had decided to latch a climb onto the trip, he congratulated me and said he had two small children who kept him and his wife on their toes. "Enjoy these times," I told him. Then I shared that Caroline and I had danced to Darius Rucker's song "It Won't Be Like This for Long." I said he should enjoy his time with his small children, even though they might drive him crazy at times. We both laughed. During the next thirty minutes, Noah spent his time going back and forth talking to me and Jim. Jim had decided to stay above rather than come down to where I was. Not a problem—he'd been through enough for one day.

Soon, I could hear the helicopter coming up the canyon. There I was, lying on the ground, staring up into the deep blue sky, knowing I was going to be involved in a helicopter rescue. While the situation was extreme, when I heard I would ride in a helicopter instead of trying to hike down, I was both relieved and excited! This was going to be cool!

My climbing group and ski buddies often joked about the "sled of shame" we would see when people hurt themselves and had to be brought down. We always wanted to avoid that. This was a completely different situation. Noah said they would "short haul" me out of the canyon and back to a meadow by the trailhead. Short hauling was designed to rescue people when they couldn't land a helicopter because the terrain is too steep, or someone is in a precarious position and can't be physically loaded into the helicopter. The process includes a basket/litter being brought into the area dangling from the bottom of the helicopter. It is lowered to the ground on a long rope and unclipped by people on the ground. Then the person being rescued is placed in the basket, the basket is reattached, and the helicopter flies off with the basket dangling beneath it. The helicopter then flies to a level spot where it can meet rescuers and an ambulance.

When the helicopter showed up, I could hear it get close to the ground. Then Noah and a few other rangers who had arrived on the scene, including Case Martin (one of the lead rangers), unclipped the basket. Case explained that the helicopter would drop the basket off, they would unclip it, and then the helicopter would leave. "Don't worry when you hear him leave. He'll be back after you're loaded." So that's what they did.

Soon, I was loaded and strapped into the basket, which was about the length of my body. Case informed me they would need to cover my eyes for a short time because of the helicopter downwash. As I was gradually lifted off the ground, with Case strapped to the basket with his legs dangling down over my right shoulder, I jokingly said to Case, "You must be my guardian angel." I'm not sure if he smiled. While the helicopter headed to Lupine Meadows, where they intended to drop me off, Case and I had a quick conversation. He said I was lucky, which was the second time I had heard that. Noah had said the same when I described to him what had happened to me. My response to Case was, "You bet, considering the fall and being able to get out because of some chance circumstances."

The trip to Lupine Meadows took fifteen to twenty minutes. When we got less than ten minutes out, he removed the cover from my eyes. The sight, while lying in a basket floating along in the sky with a guy hanging next to me, was breathtaking! I looked up to see the helicopter and eighty-foot-long rope connected to the basket I was in; Case was to my right, and the beautiful blue cloudless sky was all around. You bet I was lucky…and thrilled about the ride too!

Once we reached Lupine Meadows, the helicopter gently lowered the basket to the ground. Then Case unclipped it from the dangling rope, and we were greeted by an ambulance. While I was being put on a stretcher and getting into the ambulance, the Park Service sent the helicopter back to the fall sight to pick up Jim. He got the more exciting ride! They simply put a harness around his waist and chest; then they short-hauled him while he dangled below the helicopter. He got to look around in the valley while being transported. "It was better than any ride I experienced at Six Flags or Disney," Jim said when we were interviewed later. What a couple of knuckleheads we were! Noah had arrived on the scene where Jim and I were at 2:25 p.m. It was now after 5 p.m. (according to the incident report filed by the Park Service). Whew! Hard to believe that much time had passed.

I was quickly loaded into an ambulance and had a short reunion with Jim. Both of us were smiling, but still in shock over what had happened. In the ambulance, I was turned over to an EMT named John Politis. John is another unsung hero of our National Park System, in addition to Noah, Case, and the rest of their ten-plus member rescue team. John is considered a rescue EMT, and he told me about several rescues as we chatted in the ambulance, including one on Denali in Alaska less than two years before.

While we were talking, I said my wife would probably keep me on a short leash now because of the accident and my age. "Nonsense!" said John. "Being in the outdoors has inherent risk. You need to get back out there." Then he said I was lucky. Huh…three times during the rescue. He then explained he had said that because over the last few years, three other people had gone into the ice moat close to where I had. "You're the first rescue. The others were body recoveries because they couldn't climb out." That was a bit of a conversation stopper. It quickly brought the severity home.

In addition to those who had died while descending from the Grand, I later learned from the park rangers that there's an area at the top of Spalding Falls known as "Miller Flats." It's named for another climber who suffered a fatality.

On June 20, 2013, fifty-five-year-old Gary Miller from Colorado Springs, Colorado, was descending the Grand Teton after a successful summit. The day was beautiful, and his climbing team was descending as part of guided climb. While standing at an altitude of approximately 10,000 feet at the top of the North Fork of Garnett Canyon (close to where Jim and I were), he slipped while waiting to get the go ahead from a lead guide to proceed down. Suddenly, he was sliding down the snowfield very fast.

Once he started sliding, Miller couldn't self-arrest because his ice ax had come free from his hands when he lost his balance. After sliding a short distance, he ended up falling into an ice mote under the ice and snow, close to where I had dropped in. The guides threw a rope down to him, hoping he could climb out and save himself. They next tried multiple times to pull him out or have him climb out, but finally, because he was exhausted, all they could do was try to pull him out from inside the moat. The park ranger report states that he seemed to get caught up on the sides of the ice mote while trying to be pulled out; he most likely succumbed to hypothermia, and he died.

His story brought tears to my eyes. I feel for his family, considering my family could have experienced a similar story. It makes me realize how lucky I was to be out of the icy mote.

"When we try to pick out anything by itself, we find it hitched to everything else in the Universe."

— *John Muir*

Once I arrived at the ER at St. John's Hospital in Jackson, the pace became frantic. I was greeted by an army of ER doctors and nurses. It was like a scene from *ER* or *Grey's Anatomy*. They cut off my jacket and shirt, pulled off my hiking boots, proceeded to do X-rays and CT scans, and evaluated me from head to toe. I found out then that I had broken my left leg, had potentially detached a ligament from my knee, and had a severe bruise on my left side from my hip almost to my knee. Jim said I should call Mary to let her know what had happened. I said I would rather not. I was trying to digest everything and unsure how to explain it to her without really upsetting her and having her ask a lot of questions I didn't have answers to.

Because I had lost my phone in the fall, I finally took Jim's wise advice, used his phone to call Mary, and let her know what had happened. "I lost my phone so I'm using Jim's," I explained. "I fell while hiking and broke my leg. I'm in the emergency room and doing fine. I'll see you tomorrow." I understated the situation a bit, but I thought that would be best for now. Jim also called his wife Linda, but he told her all the details. "Never again," Jim told Linda. She replied, "You've said that before." Over the years, we had gotten lost on adventures, been significantly delayed, and experienced some tight spots. When Jim came back from those adventures, he would tell her "Never again." So, this time, she said, "Right. You two should get tattoos to remind you when you get back." We got a chuckle out of that since she was probably right.

A short time later, Mary sent a text message to Jim, asking, "If he broke his leg, how did he get down?" Jim replied, "Dangling from a helicopter." That motivated a phone call from Mary, and I fessed up to what had really happened, but again, I stressed I was okay. I also mentioned I had lost my driver's license during the fall. "How are you going to get on the plane without any ID?" Mary asked. Good question. She had the brilliant idea to fax a copy of my passport that I keep at home…if the hospital would allow it. We mentioned the dilemma to the nurse and our solution. "Not a problem," he said and promptly gave Mary the fax number. Whew! That could have been an issue. I thanked the nurse profusely.

We checked out of the hospital, then headed back to Ned and Kathryn Rawn's house for the night. While we were there, Jim had the chance to speak with Mark by phone for the first time since the accident. Jim filled him in on what had happened. Initially, we were going to connect with Mark and Nicholas after the hike, but we decided we would connect later. Jim told Mark he still had the rope he had used to save me. I would later ask Mark for the rope to keep as a memento, which he gladly gave me.

After dealing with some airline issues (could I get through security with just a copy of my passport?), I headed to bed for a restless night's sleep.

The next morning, I was up early. Jim and I said goodbye in the Rawns' driveway. I was driving the four-plus hours back to Salt Lake City's airport (fortunately, I'm a right footer) and then flying back to Atlanta; Jim was driving back to Coeur d' Alene, Idaho, to celebrate the Fourth of July with his family. Our emotions when we hugged goodbye were a bit overwhelming,

Foursquare Mountaineering. Dennis, Pete Shepard, Doug, Ron, Mark, Dan, Jim, Dave

Ascending Mount Rainier 0610. Camp #2. Ingraham Glacier.

Disappointment Cleaver – Pete Shepard

Mount Rainier – Little Tahoma on Right

Crevasse on Mount Rainier

First Summit Mount Rainier with Pete Shepard

Sunrise Mount Rainier – Disappointment Cleaver

Final Ladder climb to Three Finger Lookout Fire Hut

Three Finger Lookout (circled)

Mount Kilimanjaro summit with team and guides

Mount Kilimanjaro team – Drew, Dan, Jim, Pete, Joe, Doug, Reg, Mai (seated), Caroline

Mount Kilimanjaro Sunrise

Mount Kilimanjaro

M. McGuire Backcountry Skiing White Pass

Pete Matheson and Dan Rim Mount St. Helens

Summit Mount St. Helens – active lava dome center; Spirit Lake in distance

Looking into crevasse on the Nisqually Glacier Mount Rainier (Caroline)

Crevasse Climbing Nisqually Glacier Mount Rainier – Dave, Jim, Doug, and Caroline

Daniel and me – Cot's Peak Mount Cleman. Patchwork quilt of Yakima in background

Wenker Family photo – Jan (Dave's wife), Dave, Dan, Barb, Dad, Mom

The Family – Darby, Daniel, Caroline, Anthony, Mary, Dan

Grand Teton at night

Down climb chute from Lower Saddle Grand Teton

Nicolas and Mark McGuire

Short Haul Rescue (my ride down) – Grand Teton National Park

Valley at the bottom of the Grand Canyon

Dragontail Peak – Jim, Doug, Ron, Dan. Colchuck Lake below in background

Colchuck Lake – Dragontrail Peak (center), Colchuck Peak (R), Aasgard Pass (L)

Grand Canyon looking from the south rim to the north rim

Conclusion of successful N. Rim 2 S. Rim Grand Canyon with Reggie

Mount Kilimanjaro Summit Embrace (Joe, Dan, Caroline)

Dan/Caroline Summit Mount Adams

Mount Whitney – tallest mountain in the contiguous United States

Jim Zingerman and me. Ingles Peak (Mount Stuart in background).

Mount Hood, Oregon 11,249 ft.

Camp Sherman Base Camp

ending in a few tears flowing on my part for the first time since that glorious moment when my head popped out of the ice moat and Jim memorably said, "Good to see your face." Jim was also nice enough to give me the rescue whistle he had used to get the attention of the park ranger.

Mark and Nicholas summited that day, which was phenomenal! The next day when Mark saw Jim, he said they had seen the helicopters that had airlifted us down from the Lower Saddle while they were hiking back to the car. They had wondered if it was for a rescue. He also told Jim their descent wasn't without incident. While hiking down through the woods after the boulder field, they had encountered nine bears—some at a close distance. Two were Grizzlies and the rest were Black Bears with cubs (an extremely dangerous situation). That's all we needed—more twists to an already epic adventure!

WHAT I LEARNED

The events of June 30, 2022, remain fresh in my mind as I write. People ask if I plan to climb again and whether it's smart to continue to take chances like that. Well, we decide our path to get the most out of this one life we get.

Climbing and hiking hits many buttons for me—the preparation and physical conditioning, seeing the goal and being more than a little nervous when you see and read about the adventure you're planning to go on, friendships and bonds with the people you spend hours and days with while encountering extreme highs and extreme lows, and of course, the exhilaration of reaching a summit and making it back to the car.

As John Politis emphatically told me, "inherent risk" is part of climbing (and life). Something to consider going forward.

FIVE THOUGHTS ON ACCEPTING INHERENT RISK

1. Things that might seem risky to one person are not risky to another.
2. You must accept the risk when doing an activity.
3. Certain risks come with living your life, so should you stop doing what you love?
4. While inherent risk exists everywhere, it makes life more exciting.
5. You cannot completely avoid any risk in your life.

SUMMARY

> "You must do the thing you think you cannot do."
>
> — Eleanor Roosevelt

For me, the sense of accomplishment plays a big part in taking risks. Like EMT Park Ranger John Politiz said to me in the ambulance, "Life has inherent risk." Everyone makes their own choices on how they handle risk and how they go through life. I respect both perspectives. The risk and potentially fatal outcome did hit me hard, though, when speaking to my wife, kids, and my ninety-one-year-old dad.

Two things come to mind when people ask me, "Would you do it again?" First, I do not plan to die an early death. Secondly, how do I want to live? Do I want to live life experiencing new things that involve some risk—not extreme risk like the world-class climbers or people who are considered daredevils and "living on the edge," but a life with some calculated risk? Yes, I do—it brings joy and enables you to fully experience life and all its beauty. It also hopefully provides a mantra to my family that life should be lived to the fullest. So many people at my stage in life end up with health issues and pass away earlier than expected. I choose to do exciting, body and mind-expanding activities since we don't know what our Maker's plan is for us. My philosophy is to live life knowing I have similar chances of dying from cancer or being hit by a car as I do experiencing the thrill of the outdoors in a calculated way.

CHAPTER 10

COMING TO TERMS WITH REALITY

"Life is not a problem to be solved, but a reality to be experienced."

— Soren Kierkegaard

Have you ever had something happen to you, but a few months later, the details fade and you wonder if it really happened? Falling below the surface of the snow and climbing out of that moat sometimes seems surreal to me. When I tell the story, the words come out and I believe what I'm saying, but the actual event seems too bizarre to be real. When I tell the story, people's faces show shock and amazement, or they say, "Nah. It couldn't have been that bad."

About a year and a half after the accident, while doing research on Miller Flats and the fatal accident that cost Gary Miller his life, I came across a copy of his incident report which recapped what had happened to him. The report was chilling and again drove home how miraculous my survival was. Then I started to wonder if the Jenny

165

Lake Park Rangers had written a report on my accident. If so, what did it say? Would it state the details I was told, had experienced firsthand, and had come back to me in quiet moments when my mind wandered? I decided to reach out to Ryan Schuster, the Jenny Lake Park Ranger who had been so helpful in communicating details to me after the accident and had worked so hard to coordinate having my backpack and gear returned to me from deep in the wilderness. He told me there was an incident report on file and how I could obtain a copy. Wow! What would it say?

After a couple of weeks, the report was emailed to me. It gave the details I've shared here with a couple of minor differences. It outlined the event Jim and I had experienced and how I had climbed out of the moat with Jim's help. The report galvanized the experience with cold, hard facts, and it was written in a manner that showed little emotion (as it should). In an unemotional insert into the section marked "contributing factor," the words "judgement error" were input. Well, that kind of said it all. Again, similar to Noah stating "no judgement" on his part, it was input with kindness and a sense of forgiveness.

While they could have used the phrase "significant judgement error" or even "dumbass," the severity of my bad decision was minimized. They see accidents all the time and are sympathetic to the fact that some of us, while being in awe and grateful to be in the outdoors, often make casual decisions that can be fatal.

I feel fortunate to have received the report in an unedited form. It brings home the details that happened that day in a factual manner, proves to me it all happened just as I remembered, and drives home the reality of the situation. I'm including it here:

United States Department of the Interior

NATIONAL PARK SERVICE
Grand Teton National Park
PO Box 170
Moose, WY 83012

IN REPLY REFER TO:

9.C. (GRTE)

May 1, 2024

Daniel R. Wenker
wnkrdan@gmail.com

Mr. Wenker:

We are responding to your April 27, 2024 request for a copy of incident report NP22176955 from our Incident Management, Analysis and Reporting System (IMARS). We are authorized to make this release to you under the "routine uses" clause of the Department of the Interior (DOI) Privacy Act System of Records Notice (SORN), DOI-10.

The DOI-10 SORN permits us to release information to any of the following entities or individuals, for the purpose of providing information on traffic accidents, personal injuries, or the loss or damage of property: (a) Individuals involved in such incidents; (b) Persons injured in such incidents; (c) Owners of property damaged, lost or stolen in such incidents; and/or (d) These individuals' duly verified insurance companies, personal representatives, administrators of estates, and/or attorneys.

We are required to withhold social security numbers and tribal information numbers not belonging to you. We may also withhold information when we believe it could interfere with ongoing law enforcement proceedings; risk the health or safety of an individual; or reveal the identity of an informant or witness that has received an explicit assurance of confidentiality. The information withheld from your report falls within one of these categories.

We do not bill requesters processing fees when their fees are less than $50.00, because the cost of collection would be greater than the fee collected. Therefore, there is no billable fee for the processing of this request.

If you have any questions you may contact Erin Martin 307-739-3301.

Sincerely,

Erin Martin
Dispatcher

cc: Unredacted SAR Report

Version 4	NATIONAL PARK SERVICE SEARCH & RESCUE REPORT – Page 1							WENK6955	
SAR #:	22-23	**Park:** GTNP		**SAR Account #:**	PX.EGRTES347.00.1			**Case #**	NP22176955
Start Date:	06/30/22	**Start Time:**	1425	**End Date:**	06/30/22	**End Time:**	2000	**Day of Week:**	5-Thursday

	Subject Name	**ADDRESS**		**Phone**	**DOB**
1	Daniel Wenker	65 Swan Ct Monticello, GA 31064		▬▬▬	11/19/1959
2	James Zingerman	Insert address in this textbox		▬▬▬	
3					
4					

Subject Info:	**Age**	**Sex**		**Experience Level**		
Subject #1	62	M		3. Intermediate/Developed Skills		
Subject #2		M		3. Intermediate/Developed Skills		
Subject #3		Click		Click Here (5 choices)		
Subject #4		Click		Click Here (5 choices)		

Date Subject Contacted:		06/30/2022	**Time Subject Contacted:**		1430
Location:		Garnet Canyon - near Spalding Falls			
Coordinates:					

Notification Method:		**1 - In Person**		
Incident Type:	2 - Rescue	**Contributing Factor - 1st:**	6 - Fall	
Mutual Aid:	No	**Contributing Factor - 2nd:**	11 - Judgement Error	
Subject Organization:	1 - Unaffiliated NPS Visitor	**Contributing Factor - 3rd:**	Click Here (21 choices)	
Subject Activity:	22 - Mountaineering - Unroped	**Rescue Method - 1st:**	4 - Helicopter Rescue	
Incident Environment:	10 - Mountains, 5,000 - 15,000 feet	**Rescue Method - 2nd:**	Click Here (14 choices)	
SAR Disposition:	1 - Subject Found/Rescued	**Rescue Method - 3rd:**	Click Here (14 choices)	

NUMBER ILL or INJURED:	1	**NUMBER NOT ILL or NOT INJURED:**	1	**NUMBER of FATALITIES:**	0	**NUMBER of SAVES:**	0	**UNFOUNDED:**	0

The Following Items Are Reported Only When Incidents Involve Searches For Lost Subjects	
Search: TYPE	Click Here (5 choices)
Search: Linear Distance in Miles from PLS (blank if unknown): miles	
Search: VERTICAL DIRECTION FROM PLS	Click Here (7 choices)
Search: DURATION	Click Here (10 choices)
Search: DISPOSITION	Click Here (5 choices)
Search: HOW SUBJECT WAS FOUND	Click Here (10 choices)

Brief Summary:

On June 30, 2022 at approximately 1425 hours, while on routine patrol in Garnet Canyon, ranger Noah Ronczkowski encountered a party of 2 climbers yelling for help near the top of Spalding Falls. Daniel WENKER lost control while glissading down steep snow and fell approximately 60 feet into a moat. His partner, James Zingerman was able to lower a rope to WENKER, who climbed and pulled his way out. He was injured and hypothermic. Ranger Ronczkowski helped stabilize his injuries and kept him warm. He was subsequently rescued by helicopter short-haul and transported to St. Johns Hospital for further treatment.

Version 4	NATIONAL PARK SERVICE SEARCH & RESCUE REPORT – Page 2		WENK6955
SAR #: 22-23	**Park:** GTNP	**SAR Account #:** PX.EGRTES347.00.1	**Case #** NP22176955

TIME/COST SUMMARY	Hours:	Costs:
NPS Programmed Hours: Actual, regular hours for permanent and seasonal NPS employees.	13.83	$415.36
NPS Unprogrammed Hours: Actual overtime, hazard pay, emergency hire (AD) and unscheduled part-time, and intermittent employee time & FICA-ER.	42.83	$2,224.75
Non-NPS Hours: Volunteer, military, and other non-NPS time.	0.00	$0.00
Totals:	56.67	$2,640.11

OTHER SERVICES AND MATERIALS	Costs:
Supplies and Equipment: Non-budgeted supplies and NPS equipment replacement, including meals	$455.97
Other Services and Costs: Travel, equipment rental, contracted hourly services, Mountain Weather, etc.	$0.00
Totals:	$455.97

AIRCRAFT AND VESSEL SUMMARY

Aircraft Organization:		Aircraft Costs:	Vessel Organization:	Vessel Costs:
NPS - Air Operations Cost		$2,013.17	NPS - Vessels Cost	$0.00
Other Air Operations Costs		$0.00	Other Vessel Costs	$0.00
	Totals:	$2,013.17	**Totals:**	$0.00

Non-NPS Total:	$0.00	NPS Total:	$2,640.11	Grand Total:	$5,109.25	Total Charged to SAR Account:	$4,693.89

Prepared by:		Approved by:	
Signature/Date:		Signature/Date:	

For incidents with NPS non-programmed costs in excess of $500, the following signatures are required:

Superintendent:		Regional Director:		Approved
				Disapproved
Signature/Date:		Signature/Date:		

Narrative:

On June 30, 2022 at approximately 1425 hours, while on routine patrol in Garnet Canyon, ranger Noah Ronczkowski encountered a party of 2 climbers yelling for help near the top of Spalding Falls. He radioed me, Ranger Ryan Schuster, to advise of the situation and responded to the yells for help. At 1433 hours Ronczkowski reported that a 62 year old male, Daniel WENKER, lost control while glissading down steep snow and fell approximately 60 feet into a moat. He was in the moat for approximately 20 minutes getting doused by running water before his partner, James Zingerman, was able to lower a rope to him. WENKER climbed and pulled his way out of the moat just minutes before Ronczkowski heard their calls for help. Ronczkowski added that WENKER did lose consciousness for a undetermined amount of time after the fall, was injured and hypothermic. Ranger Ronczkowski requested a helicopter rescue of WENKER.

While Ronczkowski helped stabilize WENKER's injuries and rewarm him by placing him inside a sleeping bag that Zingerman was carrying, I requested Helicopter 35HX to respond directly to the scene from a fire that it was working on near Pinedale, WY.

At 1517 hours 35HX was in direct communication with Ronczkowski and at 1722 hours it performed a power check directly above the scene in anticipation of an attempted short-haul rescue. 35HX returned to the Lupine Meadows rescue cache and shut down while rangers finished preparing equipment for the mission. A load calculation, rescue team manifest, team briefing, and risk analysis was completed at 1550 hours. At 1600 hours 35HX began a short-haul insertion of rangers Case Marin, Phil Edmonds, and a stokes litter to the scene with Ronczkowski and WENKER. Ranger Nick Armitage served at the Spotter for the mission. At 1626 hours the rangers on scene stated that they had WENKER packaged in the litter and called for 35HX to return for short-haul extraction of WENKER and ranger Martin. They arrived

Version 4	NATIONAL PARK SERVICE	WENK6955
	SEARCH & RESCUE REPORT – Page 3	

SAR #:	22-23	Park: GTNP	SAR Account #: PX.EGRTES347.00.1	Case # NP22176955

Narrative continued:

at the rescue cache at 1634 hours.

Zingerman was approximately 150 feet above the scene and would not move down to Ronczkowski's location with WENKER. He had become unable to move safely down due to fatigue and fear of the terrain below. It was determined that the safest course of action for all involved was to extract Zingerman via short-haul. 35HX immediately returned to the scene and extracted Zingerman and ranger Edmonds from his location and delivered them to the rescue cache at 1645 hours.

At 1650 hours 35HX returned to the Meadows in Garnet Canyon to land and pick up rangers Ronczkowski and Scott Guenther. Guenther was in the area at the time of call and had staged at the Platforms Ranger Cache in case additional equipment or a ground evacuation was needed. 35HX landed at the the rescue cache at 1700 hours and all rescuers were clear of field at this point.

WENKER was transported to St. Johns Hospital in Medic 1 for further treatment.

After a debrief, rehabilitation of rescue and rescuer equipment, and cleaning of the rescue cache all parties were clear and out of service at 2000 hours.

Signature/Date: Supervisor/Date:

PHOTOS:

PHOTO NUMBER
222555522

END OF REPORT

"The power of the imagination makes us infinite."

— John Muir

Seeing the report firsthand forced me to come to terms with a near-death experience. It also brought to reality Jim's selflessness in agreeing to carry an eight-pound rope for no other reason than to be a nice guy. Little did he know that one act of kindness would ultimately come to play in saving his friend's life.

Looking at the report motivated me to do some research on Noah Ronczkowski, the ranger who had come to our rescue as mentioned on the form. I learned Noah had previously been a mountain guide in Alaska where he had successfully summited 20,310-foot (6,190 meters) Mount Denali in 2010, then made a ski descent from the top, a feat rarely achieved. His rock star, badass status skyrocketed!

WHAT I LEARNED

So, what did I learn after reading the report? It confirmed that seeing things in writing by a third party makes them very real. All the details are captured, so there isn't any discussion later about the whos, whats, and wheres.

It also taught me to forgive people when they make mistakes. Park rangers, after working in the wilderness for many years, must see so many incidents that make them shake their heads. It wouldn't be shocking if they became sarcastic and jaded everytime they saw a judgment error result in a rescue involving many people and lots of dollars. However, instead of being judgmental, they're forgiving and realize that rescuing people is just "another day at the office." They border on being guardian angels.

FIVE THOUGHTS ABOUT DRIVING HOME REALITY

1. People make mistakes, and they probably realize it; don't repunish them.

2. Seeing things in print makes them believable.

3. Having a life-threatening situation documented makes you even more grateful.

4. Heroes and angels exist.

5. Jim's actions that day reinforced how eternally grateful I am to him.

SUMMARY

"Tell me and I forget. Teach me and I remember. Involve me and I learn."

— Author Unknown

I'm very thankful for the Jenny Lake Park Rangers, both for how they rescued Jim and me that day, and for the caring, factual way they reported the accident. I'm glad I have the report to refer to. No judgment existed in the report.

I'm also thankful for the report because it reinforces how grateful I should be to have survived. I challenge you to document things in your life that seem important. I also challenge you to be more forgiving when people screw up... like I did. And finally, I challenge you to stay on guard so you never find yourself reading a National Park Service search and rescue report with your name on it.

CHAPTER 11

BEING GRATEFUL FOR PEOPLE

"No one is born hating another person because of the color of his skin, or his background, or his religion. People must learn to hate, and if they can learn to hate, they can be taught to love, for love comes more naturally to the human heart than its opposite."

— Nelson Mandela

What would be the reaction from the people closest to you if you unexpectedly died? It's a question that some ponder. Not in a negative, suicidal way, but rather in thinking what the result would be if you suddenly weren't there anymore. How would people respond to that, and would they say you were inconsequential, feel remorse, or wish they would have said more to you before you were gone?

When I got in the car and headed out to Salt Lake City, I knew I had about a four-hour drive back to the airport where I would board a flight and head home. I had a broken left leg, was severely bruised, was without a cell phone, and had aches and pains all over. I had two very heavy pieces of luggage (the result of traveling for two weeks), but I couldn't carry them because I was on crutches and had to keep weight off my left leg.

The pain from my broken leg and bruises was constant and just below uncomfortable—but steady with slow, consistent throbs. I couldn't take my pain pills since Jim (Dr. Jim) had recommended I not take them because I would be driving. I was in a rental car and would need to fill the gas tank at some point during my drive. Once I got to the airport. I didn't have a driver's license since I had put it in my pack (which was still deep in the ice moat), separate from my wallet, when we started hiking on June 28. What if I got stopped by the police? Lots of questions. Instead of getting caught up in the unknown, I decided to get in the car and start driving. At least that way, I could deal with the issues one by one.

It was a beautiful day when I left Ned and Kathryn's in Driggs. About halfway to Salt Lake City, I stopped for gas after getting some food at a drive-thru. I pulled up to the gas pump, then slowly, painfully, and deliberately pivoted on my butt in the seat to the left with no choice but to keep my left leg straight because of the cast. I used the sides of the door opening to lift myself up, and then I hobbled to the gas pump, inserted the credit card, made my fuel choice, gingerly hopped my way to the car, and filled the tank.

Once completed, I hopped back to the fuel pump, replaced the hose, and then hobbled back to the car, entering in reverse to how I had gotten out. Success! It's amazing how important little victories are when you're in a reduced capacity. I was back in the car, with a full tank and headed to the rental car agency, where I would have to deal with a car return, loading my luggage onto the shuttle, and getting my bags from the curb to the baggage check-in.

Once at the rental car agency, I was greeted by an energetic young guy who checked me in through the window without seeing I wore a cast. I told him about my challenge of being unable to carry the bags because of my broken leg. He simply jumped in, grabbed the bags, and put them in the shuttle so we could drive to the airport. Once at the airport, he called the "curb police," who routinely chase people away from the curb at airports to keep traffic moving. I was extremely disappointed he went to get the curb police, knowing the zealous ones will just tell you to drop the passenger at the curb and quickly move your car. That wasn't the case in Salt Lake City. After the rental car shuttle driver explained the situation to him, he quickly grabbed my bags, told the shuttle driver he could go, and slowly walked me and my bags to the check-in desk. Lesson learned…give people credit in unique situations.

I arrived at the ticket counter about two hours in advance of my flight since I wasn't sure how long the process of checking in with just a copy of my passport would take. At the ticket counter, I explained to the counter agent what I had and that I needed to be on the flight to Atlanta. After observing my situation, she started the work to get me checked in. Because I had loaded my passport information into my Delta Airlines profile, she checked my bags, alerted TSA at the security checkpoint about the situation, and then called a wheelchair attendant to put me in the wheelchair and wheel me to the gate. To my shock and amazement, the security agent, knowing in advance I was coming, let me through security, and I was on my way, being wheeled to my flight. I had built two hours into the process; the entire check-in process and through security only ended up taking thirty. What a relief!

Instead of heading to the ticket counter, I went to the Delta Sky Club where I could elevate my leg, grab a bite, and drink a well-earned beer. After plopping myself down in a chair across from the bar, I breathed a deep sigh of relief. Then I started strategizing how I would get to the bar for beer and some food on one leg with crutches and back to my seat with my hands full. The anxious concern must have shown on my face because, without hesitation, a guy sitting in the same area asked me if I needed anything. Another good Samaritan. He got me a beer and some food so I could lift my leg and take a few breaths before heading to the flight.

On my way out, I asked the Sky Club attendant if I could get another wheelchair and if I could use the phone since I hadn't spoken to Mary since I was in the emergency room. I wanted to let her know I was at the airport and my flight should arrive on time. The attendant didn't have to let me use the phone, but she did. Once again, I was relieved and grateful for kindness given without hesitation.

Being in a wheelchair at the airport had its advantages. Once I was wheeled to the gate, the attendant rolled me down the airbridge to the plane and helped me off. Then I hobbled and hopped my way to my seat on the left-hand aisle. Soon, an older married couple sat in the seats next to me. When they asked about my leg, I told them the short version of what had happened. They were curious and showed a deep amount of concern.

After arriving in Atlanta, I had another easy wheelchair ride to baggage claim. There the wheelchair attendant grabbed both heavy bags, then wheeled me to the curb. Since I didn't have a cell phone, he offered to call Mary so she could leave the cell phone lot and pick me up. *I'm almost there*, I thought. *It's amazing how smoothly the trip has gone, considering how worried I was when I left Jim ten hours ago.*

Mary met me at the curb with a huge hug and a smile. I felt majorly relieved not only to be back in Atlanta, but with my family. We headed to our house on Jackson Lake where we had previously planned to spend the weekend with my son Daniel, his girlfriend Darby Jenny, and four of their friends who had all flown in from Seattle to celebrate the Fourth of July. Since I had a soft cast on my leg and people at the lake had heard about the accident, I had lots of questions to answer. All of the answers seemed to minimize what had happened just the day before. I was still processing everything myself, and quite frankly, I didn't want to go into much detail—simply shrugging it off as a hiking accident. When I hugged Daniel goodnight, another wave of emotions hit me, and the tears flowed again. I don't know why, but probably, I subconsciously thought how the fall might have ended my life and I would have been gone forever, never to hug him again.

Although I was handicapped, we had a fun weekend at the lake. Since we usually have people for the Fourth of July weekend, we pretty much have the menu planned out in advance with me doing the cooking and Mary doing all of the decorating and making sure everyone is taken care of. I hobbled around the kitchen, trying to do the best I could, limiting my trips down the stairs and the walkway out to the lake as much as possible. What stands out is, again, how kind people are when you're in a tough spot.

While I was cooking, Darby would come into the kitchen to ask if she could help. "All good here" was my usual response as I tried to muscle up and not admit how difficult cooking was on one leg while hobbling around on crutches (and being scolded when I didn't use them). Darby would stand there and talk for a little while, then ask again to help in a calm, even tone. After the third request, I realized she saw I was in need and wouldn't leave until I let her help...so I finally did. What a champ!

"The mountains are calling and I must go."

— John Muir

Soon our guests returned to Seattle, leaving Mary and me home alone to visit local doctors and return to a sense of normalcy. The first stop was the orthopedic doctor so he could evaluate me, get fresh x-rays to determine if I needed surgery on my leg, and see what damage I had done to my knee. At the hospital in Jackson, Wyoming, they had told me I had broken my leg and the ligament connecting my knee was slightly torn. At the appointment in Atlanta, the doctor informed me I had suffered a complete break of the bone in my lower left leg, but my knee was intact. What a relief! I've had a few knee surgeries over the years as result of ski injuries and meniscus tears. They tend to have a longer, slower recovery than a broken bone. When he told me it was *only* a broken leg, I was thrilled...something I don't think the doctor was expecting.

From there, Mary and I went through the process of getting another phone since I had lost hope of ever getting back the one I had lost in the fall. Super! I was back in communication. When I turned the phone on and got reconnected, I was surprised by the reactions I received from the fall. It was truly heart-warming. I'm humbled and grateful for the people who responded in ways I never would have imagined. I had text and voicemail messages from June 30 from people just checking in or asking me to give them a call. Many didn't know about my accident. Over the next seven to ten days when I hadn't responded, one person's messages became more and more urgent.

My long-time buddy Michael D's messages went from "Hey, what's going on?" to "I'm not sure what I said during our last conversation, but I must have pissed you off, so sorry about that." A true friend! He didn't know what had happened, but he thought there must be a good reason for me not calling him back, and he was blaming himself. I quickly called him to let him know all the details of what had happened.

Ironically, Michael had been the first person to call me after the 9/11 attack. Since we both traveled regularly for work, he called to check on me because airline traffic was a mess and he hoped I wasn't on any of the airplanes that had crashed that horrible day. Almost every September 11, we celebrate by having a "You're the only one who called" conversation. While it was serious at the time, we now get a laugh over it. Hearing the concern in his voice in his voicemail message after my fall really brought home that I would have been missed if I hadn't made it out of that ice mote alive. It's a somber and humbling feeling.

Ned Rawn was another friend I had messages from. Since we had stayed at the Rawns' house the night before heading out, he was anxious to hear about the trip. He had wondered what had happened since Jim and I hadn't eaten the leftovers he'd left in the fridge for us after he and Kathryn went to Driggs and had let us stay at their house. Jim and I had forgotten all about the leftovers when we returned from the ER. When no one returned Ned's calls, he and Kathryn became genuinely concerned. He finally got ahold of Jim, and he knew the story by the time I contacted him.

The following week, I wrote thank you notes to all the park rangers whose names I knew at the Jenny Lake Ranger Station. I also wrote to thank everyone at the ER who had taken care of me. When I think about how many people were involved in my rescue and treatment—more than fifteen—it's humbling. While the rangers had responded to my in-person thanks with, "Aw shucks, that's what we do," I wanted to make certain they knew how much it had meant to me and my family and that it wouldn't be forgotten.

While writing the thank you notes, I called the Jenny Lake Ranger Station to get addresses. While talking with the dispatcher, Ryan Schuster, I mentioned I had released my pack while I was in the ice moat. "No problem" was his response. "Once the snow melts, we'll send someone up there to see if we can find it." Two months later, Ryan called to let me know they had found my gear intact and were drying it out. Four months after the accident, I received a large box that contained my pack and all the gear I had carried that day. Simply monumental! My appreciation for them is endless!

I also wrote a thank you note to Jim for saving me that day. He could have very easily given up when he saw me go over the cliff and into the ice mote, but he didn't. We've had some great times over the years and plenty of laughs. As you can imagine, this situation was significantly different. While a thank you note seems minimal considering that Jim saved my life, I needed to express how I felt. I told him I believed he was truly touched by God that day, expressed my sincere gratitude, thanked him for his friendship, and said that the event had created a bond that would last forever.

Even though I wrote the letter to Jim, I continued to try to find a way to recognize his heroics on a larger scale. One day, Mary suggested I call the *Yakima Herald,* Jim's local newspaper that served both Yakima and Selah, Washington, where Jim lived. When I called, I left a message that they had a hero in their area. Shortly after, Luke Thompson, a local writer for the *Yakima Herald* who was also a big hiker, returned my call. Over the next couple of days, Luke interviewed Jim and me for the article. I was glad he concentrated on Jim's heroics. Within a week, the article was published as "The Grand Rescue" in the sports section, complete with a picture of Jim and his effervescent smile.

Once the article came out, I was again touched by the responses Jim and I both received from readers. Tree Top, Inc., where I had worked while living in Yakima, was the main employer in the area. Numerous people reached out to me from the area whom I hadn't spoken to in years. All the comments were centered around first a scolding of "You need to slow down," then the most touching comments on how glad they were that the outcome was positive, and finally, asking how I was doing.

I'm sure Jim received a bunch of comments, too, since now everyone in the area knew what a hero he was. Soon after, Joe Matheson posted the article on Facebook. Once again, I received positive, uplifting comments from people all over the country saying they were thinking about me and wishing me well. Not the response I expected—since I hadn't expected any at all. My motivation had simply been to recognize the friend who had risked his life for me.

My local friends in our community on Jackson Lake (Turtle Cove) in Monticello, Georgia, also were caring and sincere in saying how glad they were that I had survived and in wishing me a quick recovery. My buddy Barney in Turtle Cove still kids me about "falling in that hole" and how glad he is that I survived. Whenever I leave town to go on a trip, he will usually tell me in a strong Southern accent, "Now don't go fall in a hole again!"

I also received cards from old friends who had heard about the accident and wished me a quick recovery. Some were friends I didn't see every day because they lived in another city, like Bob and Judy Dubach, and others I saw regularly, like Nancy and Jeff Koeppel who live in our condo building in Atlanta. It was all humbling.

WHAT I LEARNED

People genuinely care about others. People want to do good, especially for those who seem challenged or down on their luck. While you constantly read about the bad side of humanity, normal, everyday people want to do the right thing—let people know their life is important and build them up so they can enjoy life.

FIVE THOUGHTS ABOUT LEARNING TO COUNT ON PEOPLE

1. Assume the best in people!
2. If given the chance, most people will do the right thing.
3. More people care about you than you think.
4. Let people know you care when you see they're struggling.
5. Be open to accepting caring gifts from strangers.

SUMMARY

"I always prefer to believe the best of everybody; it saves so much trouble."

— Rudyard Kipling

After I processed all the kind things people did for me during my trip to and at the airport, it blew me away. Why would complete strangers agree to help me? Because people are generally good.

Such an outpouring of love and genuine affection (in some cases, even before they heard the details of my accident) is something few people get to experience while they're living. It truly touched my heart. I'm grateful for all the comments, and I wish I could communicate to everyone how appreciative I am of all their thoughts. You don't generally have conversations with people about what they think of you—that might be weird. Experiencing genuine, warm, heartfelt comments from people who said they were glad my accident wasn't the final hurrah is something I'm eternally grateful for, and I draw strength from it when life gets tough.

CHAPTER 12

RECOGNIZING LIFE'S MIRACLES

"Do you believe in miracles? Yes!"

— Al Michaels, Sports Commentator

Most of my life, I've gone to church and listened to stories about Jesus performing miracles. While I always believed the stories, I also thought miracles only happened in the past and to other people. Even when listening to catastrophic stories on the news or reading about them, I often thought the term "miracle" was simply a matter of speech people used when trying to explain the unexplainable. Never did I think I would personally experience a divine intervention I would consider a miracle.

I have a hard time technically explaining why I survived my fall in June 2022. "Aw, you were really lucky," some people will say. It's easier to say it was a miracle from God than explain how everything fell into place because of sheer luck. Many things happened that day that are hard to explain. If any of them didn't happen, my story likely would have resulted in a similar ending to the ones the rangers had told me about when they said how "lucky" I was.

The first miracle was that I wasn't injured more severely when I fell. When I went into the ice moat after trying to leap over it, I first slammed, hands and chest first, into an ice wall at the top of the moat with a fully loaded, forty-plus-pound backpack. I hit the side so hard I felt the wind knocked out of me. Then things went black. I don't remember anything after that until I was standing on the ledge in the ice moat sixty feet down from where I went in. Therefore, I believe I was knocked unconscious from the fall.

When I regained consciousness, I was standing on a ledge, fully upright, and being soaked by a raging glacial waterfall. Although my hands hurt and I felt a slight pain in my left side, I did not break any arms, my collarbone, or a leg so severely that I couldn't walk (or later climb out). Nor did I land on my head and remain unconscious. The loaded backpack, resulting in me being wider than my normal body width, probably slowed my descent by providing some resistance on both sides of the ice moat, thereby keeping me from landing full force on the ledge after the sixty-foot fall, jamming my legs into my body, or breaking my back. Had I been more severely injured, I wouldn't have been able to wrap the rope around my waist and hands and then climb out under my own power with Jim pulling up the slack while I climbed.

Later, Jim stated he wasn't able to free-pull me out because of the dead weight and his inability to set up a z-pulley system, which climbers often use for crevasse rescue. If I had been injured more severely, I probably would have succumbed to hypothermia since about sixty to ninety minutes passed from when I fell until Jim could have found someone to rescue me.

The rope! The second miracle that day was that Jim had decided to be a good guy and carry the extra climbing rope in his backpack to assist Mark and Nicholas, thereby decreasing the weight for their descent. If Mark and Nicholas had decided to carry the rope, I wouldn't have had a way to climb out as quickly, again avoiding hypothermia. Also miraculous was that after Jim heard me calling his name and made a desperate prayer to God—"I need your help *now!*"—he remembered he had the rope. If he had forgotten he had it while in a state of panic, I might have been down there too long and frozen to death or become so cold I wouldn't have been able to climb out on my own.

Plus, that Jim was able to lower the rope to the exact spot where I was standing was another miraculous occurrence. Jim said once he remembered having the rope, he started throwing it down into the hole around the area where he saw me go underground. Because of the strength of the waterfall and its updraft, the rope kept being pushed back up or to the side of where he was trying to cast it. He then started feeding the rope down into the black hole slowly, the way fishermen gradually let out line when fishing. (Jim fishes regularly.)

Even though Jim was able to get the rope to descend into the hole, the opening was long enough that he could have easily lowered it in the wrong area since he had no idea where I was underground. That the rope was lowered exactly to where I was standing in the pitch-black hole is simply mind-blowing. In addition, it came down and tapped me on the shoulder so I could feel it in the dark, grab it, and pull it to let whoever was on the other end know I was okay. That is beyond just simply being "lucky." Jim could not tell me he was dropping a rope because the waterfall beside me was so loud.

Being able to climb out of that hole was also a bit miraculous. When I released my pack and started to climb, I remembered to lean back and walk up the wall, instead of just pulling myself up hand-over-hand—dramatically reducing the amount of strength it took to climb out. In addition, as I walked up the sheer rock face at a right angle, the ice wall behind me started to angle in, allowing me to press my back to the ice wall by using my legs to create pressure and reduce the amount of strength required even more—something I had just learned in an REI rock climbing class a few months prior.

Once above the surface, the miracles continued. After Jim tied me off to a rock above, he started blowing his rescue whistle. You need to realize how desolate and isolated we were. We were in a canyon below the hiker's trail that's used to ascend and descend. Jim estimates the trail was another 200 feet above us. We were in the Grand Teton National Park's wilderness at an altitude of 10,000 feet in midafternoon when most ascending hikers and descending hikers would have already passed through earlier in the day.

Jim continued to blow the rescue whistle, even though he had little hope of someone hearing. At exactly the moment Jim was blowing the whistle, Park Ranger Noah happened to be on the trail while descending after successfully summitting. Noah thought the whistle was a bird at first (probably because he was so much higher than we were). After listening to the sound longer, he realized it was a rescue whistle. Then he heard Jim yelling for help. He could very easily have walked by and never heard the whistle, resulting in Jim and me having to spend the night exposed on a sheer rock hill to the weather. Considering how long Noah had been hiking that day—about ten hours since he started about 5 or 6 a.m., reached the Saddle late morning, had climbed up the 1,000-plus vertical feet to the summit, summitted, and was hiking down midafternoon (an ascent of almost 8,000 vertical feet), he might have been so tired he would have missed the sound of the whistle and not stopped to find us and call in the rescue helicopter.

I consider all these events miraculous, but I thought my situation was unique. I didn't want to refer to it as miraculous until I had a chance to compare my story to those of two other people who experienced life-threatening falls. Here are their stories…you will be amazed.

While watching the evening news one night in January 2023 (months after my accident), I heard the chilling story of Ruth Woroniecki, who had survived sliding down a mountain on ice in California, severely injuring herself. The similarities to my accident caught my attention and my heart. Ruth had been hiking in the mountains outside of LA on Christmas Eve 2022. She had decided to hike the Cucamonga Peak, an 8,859-foot (2,700 meters) mountain a short distance outside of LA. She figured she could do the seventeen-mile hike during the day, then be back home by the afternoon to watch some football with her dad.

However, Ruth's day dramatically changed because of one misstep on an ice patch while on her descent. Due to temperatures dropping during the day, the soft snow she had encountered on the way up had become hard and icy. While hiking down, she slipped on an ice spot—that was the last thing she remembered. When she woke, she was on the ground. She had slid 200 feet before slamming into a fallen tree.

Ruth was later told if she had missed crashing into the tree, she would have slid another 200 feet before stopping—standing the chance of gaining more speed and risking even more severe injuries or death. When she gained consciousness, some hikers were standing over her who let her know they had called for rescuers who were on the way in a helicopter because of their location deep in the wilderness. Fortunately for Ruth, the hikers found her when they did or she would have been out in the wilderness alone, with the possibility of dying from hypothermia and her injuries. Her injuries ended up being severe—she cracked three vertebrae in her neck and had a head injury so severe that the rescuers told her they could see clear through to her skull.

Because of the remoteness of the location and the steepness of the hill, the helicopter could not land close to her, so she had to walk a couple of hundred feet to the helicopter with a broken neck. Wow! What an amazing story with many similarities to my fall—even thought my injuries weren't even close to what Ruth had. She was extremely "lucky" to have hit a tree to stop her fall and to have hikers walking by where she was.

"In God's wilderness lies the hope of the world—the great fresh, unblighted, unredeemed wilderness."

— John Muir

A few weeks after hearing this story on the news, I was telling my brother about Ruth's story and its similarities to my fall and rescue. He said he had heard about another woman who had a severe hiking accident in the mountains of Central Pennsylvania.

In the winter of 2022, Beth Jones, an ordained United Methodist Minister, was hiking in the hills behind her home in Central Pennsylvania when she slipped on some snow and slid about sixty feet down a steep hill at a high speed before slamming into a tree and being knocked out. When she regained consciousness, she tried to stand and realized she couldn't.

Miraculously, Beth's cell phone had fallen out but was close enough for her to grab it and dial 911. Rescuers soon arrived. They carried her out of the wilderness, and then she was taken by ambulance to the hospital. If she hadn't been able to call for help, her injuries and the cold temperatures could have been fatal to her. As a result of her fall, Beth was hospitalized for sixteen days with twelve broken vertebrae, six broken ribs, broken bones in her shoulder, a broken orbital bone, and a broken finger, plus she suffered a concussion. The location of her phone after the fall probably saved her life.

The similarities between my, Ruth, and Beth's falls were too eerie to let slide by so I contacted both Ruth and Beth to let them know of my accident, wish them well, and ask if we could connect. I was able to connect with Beth by email, and then we spoke on the phone. Our conversation was both therapeutic and refreshing. I strongly felt she understood my situation in a way others had not. I learned she and her husband lived in Central Pennsylvania. In addition to being an ordained Methodist minister, she was a certified Nature and Forest Therapy Guide. She loved the outdoors and was starting to take very short hikes again for the first time since her accident.

It took a little while for me to finally speak with Ruth via email. I found out she and her dad had a Christian ministry in Brazil. They brought food and personal counseling to people in the favelas (slums or shantytowns) in Brazil and ministered and brought the message of hope to prisoners and the homeless in some of the most horrific surroundings. Ruth explained the reason for the delay in returning my message was the lack of dependable internet where she and her dad were ministering.

When you have something bad happen to you, you wonder why. I'm not sure I still understand why. That our three lives crossed because of our life-changing accidents is truly remarkable. My life has been enriched by hearing about what happened to Beth and Ruth, and I have been deeply touched by their ministries, helping people through very difficult situations, both before and after their accidents.

I've also had the chance to visit Beth in Pennsylvania. We've compared notes about our accidents, their common attributes, and how we deal with the day to day. I'm grateful for her friendship. I'm certain God had a hand in our miracles. If you feel all these occurrences were chance coincidences and luck, that's your choice. Luck is one thing…multiple things happening at just the right time that result in you being alive is another. I'm sticking with them being miracles and divine intervention.

WHAT I LEARNED

My accident taught me that miracles happen every day. For many, they're shrugged off as lucky coincidences that fell into place. Unfortunately, most of the time, we don't completely listen to the details—if we did, we might think about incidents more deeply. Until you have had the chance to experience a miracle yourself, I completely understand why you might be skeptical.

I also learned that people tend to be humble when a miracle happens to them. For me, it was very overwhelming. Why would God allow a miracle to happen to me? When I get into that place, I find it best not to overthink it. If you ever have the same experience, I encourage you to accept it, be overwhelmed by it, and be grateful for it.

FIVE THOUGHTS ON REALIZING HOW QUICKLY LIFE CAN CHANGE

1. Miracles happen!
2. Things happen to you for a reason—you don't always know why.
3. How you respond to a life-changing situation is up to you.
4. Take the chance to reach out to people who have had an experience like yours.
5. Be in awe of a life-changing event.

SUMMARY

"Miracles happen every day. Change your perception of what
a miracle is and you'll see them all around you."

— Jon Bon Jovi

Life is certainly made up of numerous surprises and coincidences…but are they coincidences? The miracles I witnessed during my fall—Jim volunteering to carry the rope and being able to lower it sixty feet in the dark to the exact point I was located, my not having more severe injuries so I could climb out of the ice moat, and Noah walking by at the right time and hearing Jim's rescue whistle so he could help rescue us all were incidents I would describe as miracles. If they hadn't happened, they could have changed many lives dramatically.

I challenge you to look for miracles in your life. They are there if you take the time to look for them. I challenge you to look at things that seem like coincidences and wonder whether it was luck or a miraculous event that can't quite be explained.

CHAPTER 13

GETTING MORE THAN YOU EXPECTED

"The secret of adventure, then, is not to carefully seek
it out but to travel in such a way that it finds you."

— Rolf Potts

Have you ever gotten lost, then once you realized where you were, you were glad you became "misguided." Life is full of surprises. The more time I spend in the outdoors, the more I'm surprised with the enormity of it all. The surprises I've experienced, after having a preconceived notion of what to expect on adventures, have always come when I least expected them. After they came, I was always grateful. When we hiked to the Lower Saddle and stared up at the Grand Teton, I was blown away by the sheer enormity of the mountain, along with the dramatic increase in altitude.

I'm grateful for two additional surprises that happened to me both before and after the fall into the ice moat in the Tetons. One landed me in the hospital (again). The other I would not have experienced without some pushing by a friend.

In 2021, after the global chaos of COVID-19 in 2020 and once the lockdown started to wind down, Reg Blackburn (my buddy who grew up with me on the same Philadelphia street and climbed Kilimanjaro with us) called. He said he had been thinking of hiking the Grand Canyon rim to rim and asked if I wanted to go along. We had been discussing that we each needed a new challenge since both of us had retired soon after our trip to Kilimanjaro in January 2020.

I'm embarrassed to repeat what my thoughts were about the Grand Canyon. For years, I had heard that the Grand Canyon was one of the most amazing places people had experienced. Numerous trip reports online described hiking down to Phantom Ranch, staying in the cabins at the bottom of the canyon, and then hiking back up the next day. Well-publicized guided trips will also take you down to the bottom; these include riding on mules to experience the bottom of this wonder of the world. The pictures I had seen were impressive because of the Grand Canyon's wide expanse and sheer desolation—once you got past the viewing station at the South Rim. *That looks like a one-and-done experience*, I told myself. *You visit the Grand Canyon while on your way to something else. Drive to the park, park your car, walk to the viewing station, peek, snap some pictures, then leave, having "been there, seen that."* What a moron I was!

The Grand Canyon, both mysterious and historical, is 277 miles long, up to eighteen miles wide, and over a mile deep. It has an average width of 300 feet and a minimum width of seventy-six feet; the deepest point is 6,000 feet, and it covers about 1,900 square miles. Four Empire State Buildings stacked on top of each other could fit inside the Grand Canyon. It is also the eighth greatest ravine on the planet. Guess I should have read those facts before brushing it off as another tourist attraction that people peek at, then check off their list.

Once we decided to hike the Grand Canyon, I started reading up on the undertaking Reggie had proposed. The more I read, the more excited I became. While this was not a mountain peak to conquer, the trip Reggie mentioned would be a major undertaking. Because the campsites at Phantom Ranch book out at least a year in advance, Reggie said he wanted to hike from the North Rim to the South Rim in a day. By hiking the canyon in a day, we could carry light daypacks loaded down with food and water and eliminate the need for a large pack with sleeping bags, cooking stoves, and all the stuff for an overnight adventure. Light and lean—it sounded like a good move.

Reggie started talking about parking at the South Rim, taking a shuttle to the North Rim, getting a room there, and then starting to hike early in the morning the next day. Day hike, light pack, no sleeping in tents on the hard ground—sounded great. Then I read the details while plotting how much to train for this "day hike." According to the All-Trails app, the hike from North Rim to South Rim via the North Kaibab and Bright Angel trails is a twenty-five-mile, 5,574-foot elevation gain hike that will leave hikers speechless, and it is usually done in two to four days. It can take anywhere from twelve to fifteen hours to complete if doing it in one day.

Temperatures at the bottom of the canyon can reach 110-120 degrees, even early in the season (June). I read the warnings that "People die trying to hike rim to rim in a day" and that a one-day hike was "highly discouraged." I also read how great the hike was, and a variety of posts said that if you were in good shape, going rim to rim was very doable. Done deal…we would train hard like we did for Kili and give it a whirl. "Shouldn't be a problem," we both said.

For the next three months, Reggie and I trained hard at some of the same sites we trained on in Georgia when preparing to climb Kilimanjaro, including Stone Mountain, Kennesaw Mountain, and the Kephart Prong Trail, a twenty-five-mile, 6,800-foot (2073 meters) vertical gain hike in the Great Smoky Mountains. While researching the hike and what to be aware of, I found a three-month training schedule online that people used to hike the R2R (rim to rim) in one day.

"Most people are on the world, not in it."

— John Muir

Finally, the time came in June 2021 for us to fly into Phoenix and then drive to the Grand Canyon to start our adventure. We parked the rental car at the South Rim and then grabbed the four-hour shuttle to the North Rim. We were joined on the bus by a single woman and a couple. The couple was in their early forties. They were celebrating their wedding anniversary by hiking the Grand Canyon R2R. The wife had run the canyon R2R previously; her husband was a big mountain biker and was doing it for the first time. The single woman had hiked it before while moving from Texas to Oregon. She was now doing it a second time while moving back to Texas from Oregon. She was dropped off at the trailhead in the late afternoon when we arrived at the North Rim trailhead—she intended to run the distance at night. Impressive!

Once we arrived at the North Rim hotel, we checked in and grabbed some dinner before an early night to bed. At 4:30 a.m., we woke, grabbed a quick snack, and then got on the shuttle to the North Rim trailhead where we started hiking in the dark. We started out together with the couple, but they soon left us since they planned to push for an aggressive time to complete the hike to the South Rim. It was dark and chilly when we started, but the stars were out, so it was perfectly clear. Excellent conditions for a long hike!

As the sun rose in the Grand Canyon, I realized what a knucklehead I had been for minimizing the beauty and magnitude of this otherworldly adventure. Instead of the dead, rock landscape you see in South Rim photographs, we were in a place with beauty of a magnitude I'd never seen. We passed roaring streams and lush vegetation both on the trail as we descended and while we hiked the bottom of the canyon floor. It was all I could do to keep my eyes on the trail.

As the sun came up, we looked up at the multilayered rock surrounding us on the canyon walls. Each layer contained various colors, ranging from a light tan sandstone to a bright orange and even blue rocks, as far as we could see. We hiked along a babbling stream for a while. As we came around one bend in the trail, we could see the stream's origin—a raging waterfall that dropped straight down from one of the canyon rims to the bottom of the canyon; it was about 1,500 feet high. This was not the dead monotone place I had seen pictures of and envisioned in my mind; rather, it was a vibrant ecosystem that went from a dessert at the top to a lush green forest at the bottom.

Around each corner was another mind-blowing sight where we would take some pictures and think it couldn't get any better…and then it did. While the hike up the Bright Angel trail was a bit of an emotional and physical challenge, we finished the hike in just under twelve hours. We were exhausted with a few blisters but thrilled to have done the hike in a day. I was grateful, appreciative, and humbled that Reggie had invited me to do it. After downplaying what to expect, I had learned a valuable lesson about prejudging something so many people had claimed to be the most amazing place they had experienced.

WHAT I LEARNED

This experience taught me many things—especially being grateful for surprises. I would have missed experiencing the Grand Canyon's breathtaking beauty and magnitude if not for a friend's suggestion and being willing to go on the trip—even if only for the challenge rather than the location.

I also learned you should research something if you hear it's amazing, but don't personally understand why. That way, you won't decide based on your own thoughts but rather the facts. Reg and I have a friend who has traveled all over the world yet thinks the Grand Canyon is one of the most amazing places on the planet. Hearing that should have alerted me that there might be more to it than just going to the edge to take a peek and then move on.

FIVE THOUGHTS ON GETTING MORE THAN YOU EXPECTED

1. Don't prejudge an area, activity, or adventure.
2. Research, read, and talk to people, before forming an opinion.
3. Life offers surprises—be ready for them.
4. Have friends who enjoy slightly different activities than you.
5. Embrace the unknown.

SUMMARY

> "I make myself rich by making my wants few."
>
> — Henry David Thoreau

If I had listened to my inner voice, I never would have experienced the Grand Canyon. Fortunately, when Reg called me to hike the Grand Canyon rim to rim, I said, "Sure. Why not?" We were both retired, were looking for a challenge, and it seemed like he had all the details we needed. What I didn't realize is how phenomenally beautiful the Grand Canyon is. Unless you take a chance occasionally and do something you have never considered, you'll never have the chance to experience a surprise.

It's important to have people around you who have similar yet different interests. That way, you can build on your life's experiences and do things that might not have been on your radar.

I challenge you to stay in tune with your close friends and be aware of some of the things they would like to do. Ask what excites them and what challenges they secretly hold inside. You might just uncover a beautiful gem like I did by hiking into the Grand Canyon and coming out mystified by its beauty. Finally, I challenge you not to make decisions based on your preconceived thoughts but on facts and research.

CHAPTER 14

MAKING DECISIONS BASED ON PAST EXPERIENCE

"To make no mistakes is not in the power of man; but from their errors and mistakes, the wise and good learn wisdom for the future."

— Plutarch

Do you feel as though your knowledge is built over time? Based on past experiences, we should be able to make decisions in the future that help us avoid bad decisions. But what if the experience is uniquely different from the current situation and deciding based on the past puts you in a worse situation?

Another outdoor adventure where I got more than I expected was when Caroline and I went skiing at Chamonix in the French Alps. Little did I know a five-day ski trip would turn into a five-week European adventure involving two emergency rooms, an ambulance ride, and five days in the hospital.

Caroline and I had an annual father/daughter ski trip on the books for a few years when she lived in Salt Lake City in the mid-2000s. In the winter of 2024, we decided we needed to revive that tradition. When we compared skiing in Utah to skiing in Europe, it became abundantly clear that the French Alps—specifically Chamonix—was not only a little more exotic but also more cost-effective. We decided we would go in mid-February and ski four days in Chamonix.

While researching skiing in Chamonix, we learned about skiing Vallée Blanche. The more we read about Chamonix, the more excited we became. Not only was this a beautiful town with four distinct mountains you could ski simply by taking a short bus ride, but Vallée Blanche was a ski run that started at an altitude of more than 11,000 feet (3,353 meters). It's length of just over twelve miles and an elevation descent of 8,100 feet (2,469 meters) makes it one the longest and highest off-piste (off-track or non-groomed) ski runs in the world. This trip was going to be epic!

We arrived in Chamonix on Thursday, February 15, with plans to start skiing the next day. We had hired a guide to show us around on the mountain for a day before venturing out on our own. Plans changed, though, when the airline lost my skis. They wouldn't be arriving until sometime on Friday. Flexibility is important with these types of trips, so we decided Caroline would still go on the guided trip leaving early on Friday morning. I would wait for my skis and then ski at one of the other mountains for half a day to get my legs warmed up.

My skis arrived late Friday morning. I decided to ski Le Brévent on my own. The weather was beautiful—clear skies and sunny—when I got on the ski lift.

Because of the dramatic altitude gain and it being warmer than normal in the French Alps, all the skiing at Chamonix was above the tree line. Soon, I was at the top and skiing down the mountain. While there was plenty of snow at the top (versus no snow down in the valley), the conditions would be described as East Coast conditions—hard, icy snow—versus the powdery conditions we were looking for, which would be closer to the Utah or Northwest US conditions we had become used to skiing while living in Washington or skiing in Utah.

Going up in the chair (and skiing down), you could see paragliders running and launching themselves off the cliffs to the side of the ski runs. They would gently hang in the air as they rode the thermals, eventually making their way down to the valley floor. Although I was sad not to be experiencing all this with Caroline, it was a spectacular situation—watching paragliders with beautiful, multicolored parachutes against a royal blue sky while skiing in the French Alps. After going down the groomed trails (smoothed out by snow equipment) above the tree line a few times, I decided to take a couple of runs off-piste where there was more snow, the route was less traveled, and I could catch my edges to make sweeping turns.

About the third trip down, I started skiing off-piste to the left side of the groomed trails. Fewer people were there and the snow was better. On my third trip down, I was loving life and skiing down an off-piste slope at about a forty-five-degree slope when I caught an edge while making a turn, hurling me forward and landing hard on my upper chest. That caused me to slide about twenty-five feet before gradually coming to a stop on a flat portion of the hill. *That really hurts*, I said to myself while lying flat on the ground. The fall had taken my breath away, and it was significantly more painful to my upper chest than any I had ever experienced. As I lay there by myself looking up, I thought I had probably broken a rib.

I had broken a rib years before while living in Yakima when I fell off the tailgate of a friend's pickup truck. When I went to the hospital after that fall, the doctors took x-rays and then told me, "There really isn't anything we can do. You just need to go home and wait for it to heal." So, I applied my four years gaining an Ag Econ degree and continued skiing since, "There really isn't anything you can do."

When I got back to the top of the lift, I grabbed a beer and continued to ski the remainder of the afternoon. (I would later be scolded by two doctors in two different languages for this decision.) At the end of the day, I grabbed the bus back to our Airbnb and waited for Caroline to return from her guided ski day. As I sat there drinking a beer, the pain in my chest started to build. I knew I needed something to relieve the pain, so I took four 200-mg Advil and waited. When Caroline got back to our place, she was so excited about her day skiing in Italy with the guided group that I didn't want to tell her I'd had a hard fall.

"Everybody needs beauty as well as bread, places to play in and pray in, where nature may heal and give strength to body and soul."

— *John Muir*

During the night, the pain on my left side gradually increased. I got up and grabbed a few more Advil. I still hadn't mentioned anything to Caroline. We had traveled more than twelve hours to get to Chamonix, so I wanted to ski after traveling that far. I also didn't want to cancel the guided session I had scheduled to ski down the world-famous Vallée Blanche in two days.

The next day, February 17, we woke to a beautiful day. After grabbing some breakfast and getting all our gear on (and after I downed four more Advil), we headed out and skied the day at Les Grands Monets. What a glorious day it was! While the groomed runs weren't as icy as I had experienced the day before, the off-piste areas had nice snow (not powdery, just softer snow). We were able to take in the mind-blowing views the Alps offer, grab lunch outside, and enjoy the after-ski environment at an outdoor café with some great music. Life was good.

The following day, I was scheduled to ski the much-anticipated Vallée Blanche, which is an all-day affair. When we got to the Aiguille du Midi gondola that would take me to the 12,000-plus-foot altitude, the environment was so electric it made me giddy and excited with anticipation. While backcountry skiing has become a regular activity in the US, the people around me took alpine skiing and climbing to a new level. Most people, since they were headed to the Vallée Blanche glacier, were equipped in Scarpa backcountry ski boots (lighter ski boots used for backcountry/off-piste skiing), climbing ropes, and climbing harnesses, and they were trying on their crampons to make certain they fit before heading up to the top of the gondola. Because of the danger involved in potentially falling into a crevasse or breaking through a snow bridge, most people will hire a local guide company to lead them down.

The Vallée Blanche adventure consists of meeting the guide at the Aiguille du Midi cable car in Chamonix and then riding to an altitude of 12,600 feet to start your ski down. It's the highest mountain peak served by an aerial lift system whose name translates as "Needle of the Mid-Day." Caroline had decided not to join me in skiing the Vallée Blanche but to ski another slope. However, she did join me to meet up with the guide and came with us to the top of the gondola. Once we met with our guide, who would show us the safe way down so that we didn't ski into a crevasse or over a fragile snow bridge that could collapse and result in a fall, we packed our skis onto our packs and headed up.

The ride up was mind-blowing! While we looked at the more than 12,000-foot peak where we would be dropped off, I could see all the other high mountain peaks in the Alps, including the famous Mont Blanc. While 12,000 feet is a significant height (the same height as Mount Adams—the second highest peak in the Pacific Northwest after Mount Rainier), the top of the cable car was just one of many peaks its size, including Mount Blanc at almost 16,000 feet (4,878 meters). This was going to be a spectacular ski day. We exited the cable car and then walked through a maze of underground tunnels that would lead us to the opening where we would start our adventure.

Once again, the environment in the tunnel was electric. Because the ski down Vallée Blanche entails a steep hike down to get to the glacier on a razor-thin trail at a forty-degree angle, crampons and climbing ropes are highly recommended. Our guided group of six people put on our crampons and roped up in the tunnel with numerous other skiers. We then slowly walked to the cave opening where the Alps and the enormous glacier we would ski down opened to us like you would see when exiting a deep coal mine. Slowly, deliberately, we worked our way down a trail less than one-foot wide while our guide remained in the back, holding firmly onto the rope that connected our group. After twenty-five minutes, we reached a flat spot at the bottom of the steep trail at the glacier's top. At that point, we shed our crampons, clicked into our skis, and prepared to ski the 12.4-mile, 9,200-vertical-foot (2,804-meter) descent down the Vallée Blanche. I could hardly speak I was so excited. This was a "big boy" ski.

We followed our guide down, staying close enough to follow his path without crowding. While I skied down, it was hard to concentrate and keep from looking around in awe of my surroundings. After skiing down one pitch, and just before we started passing through one of the treacherous areas that contained numerous crevasses, I went to turn and either because of a concentration lapse or because my body didn't respond due to my aching ribs, I once again caught an edge and fell hard onto the ground, causing my skis to release. I landed just in front of a gaping crevasse. Whew! "That is not a good place to fall, monsieur," the guide said when he turned around. Because of how hard I had hit, my side started hurting more and I heard a low "Pop!" when I landed. Fortunately, I had taken my now regularly scheduled Advil just before getting on the cable car.

From there, we skied down without incident, including stopping for lunch at a flat spot. It was one of *the* most impressive lunch spots I've ever experienced while skiing. All around us was the beauty of the Alps, with their monumental peaks, dramatic spires jutting straight into the air, huge seracs the size of small busses, and gaping crevasses. After a restful lunch, we proceeded down to the bottom of the Mer de Glace glacier.

At that point, I remembered what I had read in preparation for the ski. Because of the glacier's constant melting, it is necessary to hike up 380 steps so you can get on the Mer de Glace train, which will drop you off in downtown Chamonix where I was scheduled to meet Caroline. When we got to the base of the stairway, I removed my skis and attached them to my pack.

At that point, I looked up to what seemed like a hike to the heavens. Then I slowly started my trek to the top. After going up a few levels, I realized I was getting more winded than usual. "Shoulda worked out harder to prepare," I grumbled. (Later, I would find out the reason I was so winded.) After getting off the train, our team got together, returned our transmitter beacons (used as safety devices in case you fell into a crevasse on the way down) to the lead guide, and said our goodbyes. Before saying goodbye, I picked up my skis that I had laid on the ground. Again, I heard a pop and felt a stabbing pain in my side. This time the pain was more severe, so I lay down flat on a stone wall while waiting for Caroline to come.

In about thirty minutes, Caroline arrived as perky as ever. She had spent the day skiing one of the other mountains, and she was ready for a beer and dinner. When she arrived, I said, "I'm not doing so well. I think I need to go to the emergency room." I then confessed completely about the fall and my two-day Advil remedy. I said the side where I thought I broke a rib was hurting more, and I couldn't raise my left arm above my waist.

After a quick Google search, Caroline found a hospital with an ER about 1.5 miles away. After calling for an Uber (which didn't show up) and going to the empty cab area, we decided to walk to the emergency room. Caroline grabbed my skis; I was in my ski boots with my pack on, and we started walking through the scenic neighborhoods of Chamonix, eventually arriving at the hospital. The sign on the door said they closed at 7 p.m. Whew! Glad we arrived around 4:30 p.m. Now to go in and see what exactly was going on.

That's when being in a foreign country hit us hard. When we checked in at the desk, a small, nice French lady greeted us in French. *"Bonjour!"* she said, looking at our wide-eyed expressions. *"Parlez-vous français?"* Caroline put her thumb and index finger closely together to indicate "a little." I was completely in the dark. After some gestures and a short game of emergency room charades, we let her know I thought I had broken a rib and needed x-rays. She was phenomenal! Neither of us spoke the other's language, but we managed to check in and see a doctor in a short time. The doctor took me down the hall to the x-ray room.

Caroline stayed in the ER waiting room with my skis, backpack, and some ski gear. In what seemed like no time at all, the doctor came out and started speaking French with the x-rays in her hands. While the language challenge set in again, a woman on the other side of the waiting room said she could translate for us. She was sitting with her son who had injured his wrist snowboarding. The doctor explained, via our translator, that I had severely broken three ribs and I had fluid behind the ribs, but a CT scan would be needed to identify the issue.

However, they didn't have a CT scan machine at the Chamonix hospital. The doctor said an ambulance would take me to the hospital in the next town so I could have a complete evaluation done. This was becoming more involved than I had expected and was challenging my "You can't do anything about broken ribs" belief. I was wheeled on a stretcher to an ambulance the size of a sprinter van where two French paramedics (who spoke no English), Caroline, and I headed off on the forty-minute drive down to the larger town of Sallanches—a small commune with a population of less than 20,000 people (Chamonix's population is less than 10,000).

We arrived at the ER in Sallanches in the dark, not having any idea where we were. We only knew we were in a French hospital slightly larger than the one in Chamonix. The nurse who greeted us immediately started an IV and let me know he would be giving me a shot of morphine. Spectacular! The Advil I had been taking was wearing off and my pain was starting to spike. After another series of x-rays and a CT scan, I met with a doctor in the ER who confirmed I had broken three ribs and suffered a pneumothorax (collapsed left lung) because of being punctured by my broken ribs. Flashbacks from my Jackson, Wyoming, ER visit after the Grand Teton experience came rushing in.

She explained (again in broken English/French) that I needed to have a tube inserted into my chest above my left breast and then into my lung to start pumping out the liquid. She anticipated I would be in the hospital for four days. Then she casually stated I couldn't fly for thirty days and wasn't allowed to lift anything over five pounds. Later, I learned flying with a collapsed lung can be life-threatening due to the difference in air pressure between the ground and a plane's cruising altitude. The air trapped in the chest expands as the plane ascends, which can severely worsen the condition. My look of confusion was noticeable as I asked, "Thirty days?" "*Oui, monsieur,*" she replied.

Caroline and I looked at each other and started to laugh—half-nervously, half-humorously. "I guess this is the European vacation you've been talking about, Dad," Caroline said with a twinkle in her eye. We told the doctor we wanted to call a friend of Caroline's in the US to ensure we had heard everything correctly. The doctor completely understood. We called Asante, Caroline's high school friend in Miami who is a doctor; she confirmed that was the correct procedure for the diagnosis. What the doctor in the ER didn't know was Asante is a gynecologist. (You can't make this stuff up.)

Learning from my last ER experience after an accident, I asked Caroline to call Mary to let her know what had happened and that I couldn't fly for thirty days, effectively resulting in me having to stay in Europe for the next month. Mary and Caroline decided Mary would fly to Chamonix (one way since we didn't know when exactly I could leave) so Caroline could return to the US and work.

The ER doctor inserted a tube into my punctured and collapsed lung. Then I was checked into the hospital. By then, it was 11 p.m. What a day! After I arrived in my room, Caroline headed back to the Airbnb. At that point, reality hit me about the surreal surroundings I was in. I had spent the day skiing one of the most iconic off-piste runs in the world. My day had started with flowing-over anticipation. After a fall while skiing, and then going to the

ER in two small French villages, I was checked into a French hospital after undergoing a procedure that placed a tube in my punctured and collapsed lung while suffering from three broken ribs. Based on what I could tell, very few people spoke English, and I spoke zero French. While lying in the hospital bed with my mind racing about my situation, I finally fell asleep.

WHAT I LEARNED

Having a severe accident that puts you in the hospital in a foreign country could be a horrible experience. Instead, I was about to spend thirty days in a country I never would have experienced otherwise.

FIVE THOUGHTS ON MAKING DECISIONS BASED ON PAST EXPERIENCE

1. Listen to your body when it's talking, and act accordingly.

2. Each circumstance is unique—approach it that way.

3. Don't get so caught up in the experience that you disregard logic.

4. Don't make a medical decision unless you're qualified.

5. Unexpected things happen; look for the silver lining.

SUMMARY

"Just be. Let your true nature emerge. Don't
disturb your mind with seeking."

— Sri Nisargadatta Maharaj

Take an experience for how it is first presented. The opportunity to spend a few days with my daughter was awesome, even if it was in a country I had zero plans of visiting any time soon. France was low on my list.

Making the decision to continue skiing was probably not one of my best. I should have listened to the pain and had it taken care of right away. However, then I would have missed out on an experience few people have. Weighing the risk and the benefit is probably a good idea. Ask yourself, "Is this wise?"

I also challenge you to take that trip with your daughter or son—even if it's to a place you didn't plan on going. I challenge you to weigh the risks when something bad happens. Finally, I challenge you to take a deep breath if you land in the hospital injured, and try to find a positive.

CHAPTER 15

ACCEPTING LIFE CAN CHANGE

"Don't wait for the perfect moment.
Take the moment and make it perfect."

— Aryn Kyle

Have you ever run into an experience that, at the time, you thought was devastating, but when it played out, it was one of life's blessings? When life throws you curve balls, how you react is critical to how they affect you.

After experiencing three broken ribs along with a punctured and collapsed lung because of a ski accident, I ended up in a French hospital. Very little (if any) English was spoken, I wasn't sure of the level of care I would receive, and I wondered how much the experience would cost. When I woke the next morning, I looked out the hospital window from my bed. I could see the emergency helicopter pad outside, along with a stunning view of Mont Blanc. Unique situation; phenomenal view. If you love mountains and are going to be in a hospital, this is the place to be!

On Thursday, February 22, after four days of phenomenal professional care, even though my ribs still hurt, I was informed that all the fluid had been removed from my lung and it was healing nicely. I could finally check out of the hospital. Super news! The release was conditional, though. While giving me the final evaluation (in broken English), the doctor again stressed I could not fly for thirty days while the lung healed, couldn't lift anything over eight pounds, and wasn't allowed to go above an altitude of 1,000 meters (3,000 feet). Glad to be out of the hospital, I wondered how I was going to travel if I could only carry so little an amount.

After a short cab ride back to Chamonix, I found the new Airbnb Caroline had found. (We'd had to check out of the first.) I was greeted by Caroline and a welcoming Mary. (I hadn't been sure how Mary would respond when she saw me, considering my other accident in the Tetons.) Caroline was a true lifesaver after moving all our gear from the first location to the second and then setting us up with food and the basics to last us the next ten days. She left for New York the next day after giving Mary and me a quick primer on the French rails system and Booking.com.

Mary and I would be in France (the doctor recommended that since my instructions and injury summary were in French) for at least a month until I could visit another hospital and get the "all clear" to fly. While excited about the journey, we were both a little anxious about how we would get around in a country we didn't know, hadn't planned on visiting, and where few people spoke English. We also wondered how the broken ribs and healing lung would handle the travel. Now began the adventure within the adventure. Caroline and I had planned to ski for five days in France and then head home; now, Mary and I were going to spend a month in France!

And what a month it was! We decided to visit a few towns, after consulting with Caroline before she left and then on the phone after she returned to New York. Our trip wouldn't be without challenges, though. Because of my travel restrictions from only being able to carry a small amount of weight, Mary would have to carry most of our luggage. While she laughed it off by saying she was my "sherpa" for the next month, I knew she was not looking forward to it. Being the good sport she is, I was assured she was up to the task! During our month-long visit, we stayed in four cities and had one of the best vacations since our honeymoon! No strict travel itinerary, no pressure. Just the chance to see France casually and get to know the people and culture. We were like two college kids on a study abroad program…except we had the financial advantage of being able to stay in "normal" Airbnbs and hotels instead of hostels.

Our tour took us from the Alps and stunning mountains of Chamonix to Lyon—the culinary capital of the world—down to the Mediterranean coast to experience Marseille and Cassis, and then finally to Paris. After another general physician's evaluation, more x-rays, and visiting a radiologist in Paris—five weeks after injuring myself—I was given the green light to fly again. While I was excited to get home, I was a bit sad for the adventure to end. Mary and I had the vacation of a lifetime living carefree in a foreign country, eating great food, drinking spectacular wine, and meeting the most warm and hospitable people. How would our reentry into the "real world" affect the newfound reignited love we had found for each other?

The French people, their food, and their culture were spectacular surprises. I'm embarrassed to say I never had a desire to visit and travel through France (much like my thoughts about the Grand Canyon before hiking it). I had planned to ski for a few days, then go home, never having the chance to see the "real" France and change my preconceived notion of what France was about. While the scenery and the culture were impactful, the people are ingrained in my mind forever. All you hear about in the US is how rude and curt the French are. How wrong that is!

While flying home, I wrote down the specific people who stood out while we were traveling through France and had a direct influence on our adventure. The number blew me away—our lives had been beautifully influenced by approximately forty people! Everyone from the hospital staff who were always cheerful and happily worked through the language challenge; to the older gentleman in the train station in Lyon who saw we were lost and confused, so he grabbed our hand and walked us to the correct train platform, then pointed to which direction to head; to the hotel staff in Paris who went out of their way to find a doctor so I could get evaluated and gain approval to fly; and the Uber driver on the way to the airport who got us to our plane, even though I had plugged the wrong address into the app.

"Keep close to Nature's heart...and break clear away, occasionally, and climb a mountain or spend a week in the woods. Wash your spirit clean."

— John Muir

In all this magic and beauty, one thing happened while we were in France that had a monumental emotional effect. After getting checked into the hospital on February 18, I called my ninety-three-year-old dad to let him know what had happened. My dad and I were very close, and we spoke often, no matter where I was geographically. Even though his physical health had declined over the years, his mental capacity was still as sharp as ever. He thanked me for calling, wanted to hear the details, and was his usual upbeat self. By the time I checked out of the hospital and called him from the Airbnb on February 22, I could tell something was off. Whenever I would call, we had the same greeting. I'd ask, "How are you doing, Dad?" He'd reply, "Doing great," even though he was wheelchair-ridden and couldn't get out of bed on his own.

On Thursday, when I called to update him on my status, his response was, "Not so good, Danny." My brother told me his health had declined, and he had informed his doctor that he didn't expect to live longer than a few weeks. Upon hearing that, our family rallied in a way that moves me to tears while writing this.

Caroline spoke with my two nephews, who let her know (since they had visited my dad during the week) that they didn't expect him to live longer than a few days. Caroline and Daniel huddled up. Then Daniel decided to fly to New York the following morning from Seattle so they could visit my dad during his last days. Daniel arrived in New York in the evening. Then Caroline, Anthony, and Daniel immediately drove from New York to Warminster, Pennsylvania, to visit my dad at the assisted care facility where he lived. When they visited him that Friday night, they knew he was sinking quickly. Since I couldn't fly because of my injuries, we planned to Facetime with my dad the next day, Saturday, February 24.

While Mary and I were standing in an alley just off one of the main streets in Lyon, France, because of the sense of urgency and to find a quiet place where we wouldn't be disturbed, the six of us got on a FaceTime call so Mary and I could talk to my dying father. What a magical conversation it ended up being. We talked like we had all the time in the world, and we had a few laughs along the way. We told my dad how much we loved him. He replied, "I know." At the end, he waved goodbye like you normally do on a live call. Little did I know that wave we exchanged from halfway around the world would be the official wave goodbye to the greatest man I've known and my mutually agreed-upon "best friend."

My dad passed away a little over a week later in his bed. My brother was by his side as he breathed his last breaths. While it still saddens me not to have been there during my dad's last moments because of a silly ski accident, I take comfort in knowing we had a great relationship. We talked frequently, sometimes daily, by phone. A few months earlier, we had the talk about our relationship. Even though we were in good standing, I wanted to ask the question to make certain there wasn't anything lingering. During our conversation, I asked, "So, Dad, are we good?" "We're more than good, Danny," he replied. I am comforted by that memory when whispers of remorse come into my head. That warm little wave he gave me during the Facetime call is permanently etched in my brain…and it makes me smile.

WHAT I LEARNED

Prejudging a place, people, or culture could cause you to miss out on some of the greatest experiences you could have in your life. That month in France turned out not only to be a great adventure but the chance to refresh why I had married my wife thirty-six years prior.

It also taught me to accept a gift when it's given to you. Yeah, everyone says spending a month in France isn't all bad. However, some might have freaked out about not being in control. It's not easy to accept an unexpected twist in life. Finally, I learned to have candid conversations with loved ones when the opportunity arises. It might just eliminate regret down the road.

FIVE THOUGHTS ABOUT ACCEPTING LIFE CAN CHANGE

1. Prejudging without having all the facts might cause you to miss out.
2. Control what you can control.
3. When accidents happen, they might be for a reason.
4. Humility and acceptance can break a language barrier.
5. While death is sad and final, memories are eternal.

SUMMARY

> "If you want to conquer the anxiety of life, live
> in the moment, live in the breath."
>
> — Amit Ray

Life happens when you least expect it, so be ready to accept a gift. (In this case, an unplanned marriage refresh trip to Europe with my wife.) The unexpected also reinforces that you don't know when your time will be up on earth or where you'll be. No matter what your age, when the time is up, it's up for you or a loved one. Clear the air in person while you can. While I've always been a planner (and still am)—to the extent that it drives my wife crazy—I've become more open to accepting misdirection from God and being grateful for it when it comes. Change, of course, happens for a reason—so look for that reason.

Your challenge should be to always be aware when you do something hesitantly. A small gold nugget may just be waiting for you. I challenge you to be aware when something tragic happens while on a trip you expected to be joyful. Tragedy can sometimes bring joy.

CHAPTER 16

UNCOVERING THE NEXT CHALLENGE

"Sometimes the people around you won't understand
your journey. They don't have to…it's not for them."

— Joubert Botha

Do you have your to-do list? While the term "bucket list" has become popular, probably because of the movie by the same name starring Jack Nicholson and Morgan Freeman, I've never been a bucket list fan. Not that it doesn't work for a lot of people; it gets them thinking and excited about things to do and strive for. Based on what I've experienced, however, having too specific a list can be limiting. Don't get me wrong; I do have my list of climbs and adventures, which includes numerous mountain peaks all over the world. I started the list years ago. It includes Mount Ararat, Turkey; Mount Aconcagua, Argentina; Machu Picchu, Peru; and Angel's Landing, Utah; but it also includes Zion National Park and Canyonlands in Utah. All of these are places I jot down to remember when they come to mind, or I suddenly see them, and they look like cool spots. They used to be goals, and I've targeted them for years. I'm not sure now if they will happen. They are good-to-haves, but not must-haves to find self-actualization.

Mount Ararat is high on the list not just because it's a mountain to climb, but because of its historical and spiritual significance. The area's uniqueness also draws me to it in ways hard to explain. Mount Ararat is in far eastern Turkey, very close to the Iranian border. It consists of two dormant volcanoes, Greater Ararat and Little Ararat. Greater Ararat is the highest peak in Turkey with an elevation of 16,854 feet (5,137 meters). The location alone makes it somewhat of a high-risk adventure since a few climbers have gotten misdirected and ended up in Iran, causing multiple, non-climbing related problems. There's an easy fix to that, though. Numerous local guiding companies with years of experience offer guided trips up Mount Ararat, and they have excellent track records.

What draws me to Mount Ararat, in addition to the challenge of climbing a high peak, is its history. Legend and scientific study have stated that Mount Ararat is the spot where Noah's Ark landed after the biblical flood that occurred about 2350 BC. While it sounds hokey to some, it intrigues me. Based on archeological findings, there is even a spot you can visit where it is theorized the ark landed. You don't have to believe it; that's fine. If I can believe in miracles, I can buy into the theory since not believing it tends to limit the power of the God I believe in. So, I have multiple reasons to visit Mount Ararat, and it fits the category of an adventure. Adding to that are the nearby Kackar Mountains, which offer phenomenal skiing. Dream list…yes.

But it's an example of being flexible with the lists you create. It's a big world. Most of the time, you don't know what you don't know.

Mount Everest is known to be the holy grail for many climbers and those who want to set bodacious goals. It's on many people's lists because it's the highest and biggest in the world, plus it's one of the Seven Summits. For many climbers, whether technical or alpine, it represents the pinnacle of success and accomplishment. I can truly understand why. At 29,032 feet (8,849 meters), it represents the top of the world at an altitude that many jet planes cruise.

An expedition to climb Mount Everest typically takes fifty to sixty days since it requires a disciplined acclimatization process. The ideal window of opportunity is from April to June. Mountaineering teams will usually start their attack on the summit in mid-April with the goal of summitting in mid-June. Between 1990-2005, the success rate to summit Mount Everest was 1-3 percent, but it has been as high as 60 percent in the last decade. In 2023, the average success rate for climbers was 52 percent. It's estimated 600 people reached the top of the world in 2023, including 350 Sherpas, the true heroes of Mount Everest. The year 2023 was also marked with a significant death toll—seventeen climbers and Sherpas were confirmed dead or missing/presumed dead. In 2024, the average cost to climb Mount Everest was $53,448 to $59,069. However, the cost can climb to as much as $220,000, depending on travel, permits, insurance, supplies/gear, and logistics.

Cost is also determined by the route you choose (north or south side of the mountain) and if you decide on a guided or non-guided expedition. It is a long, arduous process that pushes people to their limits physically and mentally.

Just to get to the base camp at 17,598 feet (south) or 16,900 feet (north) is an accomplishment considering the long hike in and chance of sickness. To have summitted Mount Everest, considering the cost, investment of time (both in training and the actual expedition), along with the risk of losing your life and the toll it pays on people's personal lives, is a monumental accomplishment that should be respected.

"The clearest way into the Universe is through a forest wilderness."

— John Muir

Over the years, a few people have asked if I had Mount Everest in my sights to climb. The question is often from people who don't climb or spend a lot of time in the wilderness. My answer at this stage of my life, and because of recent developments involved in climbing Mount Everest, is "I don't have any desire to." My reasons are personal and should not minimize the accomplishment.

One reason I climb is for the solitude and gratification of climbing with a small team of people who have a significant goal in mind, have trained hard, and respect the outdoors. Mount Kilimanjaro can be a crowded climb if done in the peak season during the summer months (northern hemisphere). When we decided to climb Kili, we decided to do it in the early winter months from January to March. That timing is supposed to offer you the same weather as climbing in the summer (although that didn't apply in our case) without the large crowds you can encounter in the summertime.

In looking at recent pictures of Mount Everest during climbing season, you can see unbelievably long lines with hundreds of people waiting to summit a short distance from the top. Because there is one way up and one way down, it causes a traffic jam that includes respected climbers who realize the severity of what can happen and people who are there to "check the box" so they can brag to their friends at a cocktail party. The serious climbers tend to be polite and respect others attempting to climb; the box checkers are usually self-absorbed (one documentary I saw showed a lady trying on her crampons for the first time at the 17,598-foot base camp).

Many casual climbers have not properly trained or have little experience at high altitude. Unfortunately, some of these casual, bucket list climbers literally freeze to death; their body shuts down and they die while waiting in lines to summit or come down, especially if bad weather rolls in.

Putting my life at risk and being in control of my destiny is something I choose. Being at an altitude in an area called the "death zone" because of its height and your body eating itself as it screams to survive with people who don't respect the mountain or the people around them is not something I choose to do. Again, my personal perspective—especially at this stage of my life. Personally, I have too much mountaineering experience to play Russian roulette while waiting in line near the summit of Mount Everest. Falling into an ice moat taught me to stay on guard, and one can't be on guard if trapped in a line on a ridge.

Much to my family's wonder, amazement, and concern, summiting the Grand Teton remains on my target list. When I see that peak and think of the day that pivoted my life in a subtly different direction, my mind wanders and wonders, *What if?* I'm mesmerized by the Grand Teton's jagged, snowcapped peaks and awesome beauty, which I respect immensely. My desire to climb it may come from a feeling that I should respect it and try to summit it so I have a more positive memory when I look at it. My other thought is, *Do I want to climb it as an "unfinished business" goal since I tried and didn't succeed?* It almost calls me, though, and gives me the pointed, rolled index finger when I look at its stunning size and beauty. Either way, it continues to whisper to me whenever we ski in the area or when I see pictures of it in photos and online. I wish I could get it out of my head, but I can't.

Will it happen? Who knows if it will or not. It is one of the motivators that keeps me doing a workout routine to make certain I remain in good condition in case I decide the answer is yes and gear up a conditioning routine. It also fits into my every five-year challenge when I turn sixty-five shortly. Is it foolish? Should I do what Jim and I discussed before we left the Lower Saddle before the accident—become day hikers and enjoy the outdoors that way going forward? With both of our kids married, there's a chance grandchildren might be around the corner. Should I risk not being around to see them?

Risk and fear are things people live with every day. Should fear of a fatal accident drive you away from something that seems to fulfill you? People fear all kinds of things—heights, flying, water, snakes. Some face the fear and don't let it affect their lives. Others let it dominate their decisions, and as a result, they miss out on some phenomenal experiences. Ways exist to lessen the risk to climb the Grand Teton, including going with one of the professional guiding companies. The guides, as I found out on my first trip up Mount Rainier, are experienced, talented, and act as coaches and safety backup. That's what I'm considering this time to reduce the risk. We'll see how that plays out.

WHAT I LEARNED

There will always be another mountain to climb or challenge to attack. In my life, challenges keep me dreaming and push me to think "What if?" versus "Not anymore." Challenges don't always have to be the pinnacle of that activity. If you challenge yourself—for whatever are your own personal reasons—that should be more than enough reason.

FIVE THOUGHTS ABOUT THE NEXT CHALLENGE

1. Choose your own personal way to push yourself—even if it's not recognizable to all.
2. It can always be out there. Sometimes it happens; sometimes it doesn't.
3. Keep others in mind, but be comfortable with *your* challenge.
4. If people see you taking on challenges, it might cause them to do the same.
5. Make certain to enjoy the current challenge before proceeding.

SUMMARY

"After climbing a great hill, one only finds that there are many more hills to climb."

— Nelson Mandela

I struggle with making certain I'm not being self-absorbed or insensitive to the people who care about me. Is it irresponsible to take on challenges that some think are risky when, in the grand scheme of things, they're really not? Talking it through and trying to explain the motivation and what makes up our internal drive is difficult.

I'm fortunate Mary has been supportive all along. Is it better to play it completely safe at this point because of one harrowing incident, or to use the experience of the accident to lower the chances of it happening again by making wise decisions and keeping your blood flowing by continuing to challenge yourself? It's a delicate balance that will take some discussion and consideration. The important discussion needs to be had with your life partner so the two of you can decide what level of risk you're willing to take as a family.

I challenge you to find activities or set goals that make your heart beat a little faster, push you to investigate something new, or cause a little angst. I also challenge you to stay on your guard and don't put your life in an unreasonable risk position.

CHAPTER 17

LIVING WITH FEAR VERSUS AVOIDING RISK

"Don't be pushed around by the fears in your
mind. Be led by the dreams in your heart."

— Roy T. Bennett

Do people who do risky things have any fear of bad things happening? Said a different way, do people who fear something think they are avoiding any risk in their lives by not doing those things? The definition of fear is "an unpleasant emotion caused by the belief that someone or something is dangerous, likely to cause pain, or a threat." Risk is defined as "the possibility of something bad happening. Risk involves uncertainty." In both definitions, you see "the belief" and "the possibility." Not certainty but rather something in our minds perceives a chance that something bad may happen. I believe risk and fear live in a similar place.

While skiing in the out-of-bounds backcountry area at White Pass Ski Resort in Washington with Mark McGuire one winter, I had an epiphany because of something Mark said as we reached the point we wanted to ski down from. During this trip, we were trying to get to a high point on a ridge at the top of a very steep ascent around sixty to seventy degrees straight up a snowy mountain face.

The ascent was so steep that we needed to unclick our boots from our skis and hold them over our heads perpendicular to our bodies. From there, we would slam the skis into the snow sideways above our heads and take two steps, one foot over the other, by slamming the toes of our ski boots into the hillside. After we repeated that a few times, I asked Mark, "Should we really be here?" His response was enlightening. "I don't want to die either, Dan." I realized although I was fearful about where we were, Mark, from doing it before, was not as fearful and didn't feel it was overly risky. Fear and Risk.

Once we reached our goal at the top of the ridge, we found a flat spot, clipped into our skis, and had a mind-blowing ski down in calf-deep, untouched, fluffy, powdered snow under crystal-clear, royal-blue skies. If we hadn't taken the chance, that wouldn't have happened. Without Mark's experience, I never would have had the experience. His experience and risk assessment—based on knowledge—allowed us to overcome our fears and ski down without incident. Could bad things have happened? Yes. Was there a high probability based on Mark's knowledge? No.

People fear many things. When Jim and I decided to hike down from the Lower Saddle of the Grand Teton instead of climbing up, we felt we had assessed the risk because of the fear we'd had about summiting in those conditions. Just before we started down, we talked about how we were now in our sixties so maybe it was time to crank things back a little and reduce the chances of bad things happening by doing "less risky" things. "Maybe we just start enjoying some great day hikes" was the crux of our conversation. A short while later, we experienced a life-threatening event—even after making the "safe" decision. So, did we follow our fears and avoid risk?

Looking back, the injuries and near death I experienced both while skiing in Chamonix and while descending the Grand Teton was not because of risk but needless risk. It was not because of lack of fear. I am constantly fearful when doing challenging things—that's part of the excitement and what makes the victory so satisfying. Fear is a good thing because it can keep you from getting hurt. Both of my situations were caused by not being on guard when a fork in the road came, offering the opportunity to assume too much risk.

My doctor in Atlanta, Dr. Brendan Black, explained my situation in real terms that helped me better understand. When I mentioned the concern my wife had about the activities I had chosen to do, he told me I should continue to aspire to climb mountains and ski. Both activities pushed me to be in good physical condition and promoted a healthy lifestyle, which he thought was good. However, he went on to say my decision-making once I encountered a challenge in the outdoors needed improvement. He also brought age into the equation. If you make a bad decision when you're in your twenties or thirties, the recovery and risk of very bad things happening are less impactful than when you're in your sixties. The two examples are obvious when you break it down that way.

*"When we contemplate the whole globe as one great dewdrop,
striped and dotted with continents and islands, flying through
space with other stars all singing and shining together as one, the
whole universe appears as an infinite storm of beauty."*

— *John Muir*

While descending from the Lower Saddle, we decided to glissade. No problem—people do that all the time. We listened to Park Ranger Noah when he said to make certain we could see where we were going and to control our speed. We thought we had done both of those things. The unwise decision came when I decided to use my hiking poles to control my speed instead of taking the extra few minutes to unpack my ice ax so I would be able to "self-arrest" like I had been trained, using the proper equipment available.

The excessive risk-taking while skiing in Chamonix happened when I decided to keep skiing even after I had correctly diagnosed broken ribs when I fell. The properly applied fear decision would have been to stop skiing once I thought I was injured and to have the injury attended to so a possibly worse injury could have been avoided. Once again, while skiing is risky, the level of risk and potentially worse injury occurred when a certain amount of fear was not applied to make a wise decision to stop skiing and seek some medical attention.

Jim's wife had a good idea when she suggested tattoos for Jim and me so we would make wiser decisions in the future. However, instead of "Never again," my thought was to get a tattoo on my wrist that said, "Weigh the risk." That way when decision time comes, you can do your checklist and be *on guard* to make certain if the risk is minimal at first. When that second decision comes (in my case taking out an ice ax), keep your guard up and continue to evaluate pluses and minuses, thereby lowering your chance of a bad accident occurring.

So, here's the point; the purpose of my book is *not* to scare you into not doing things because a couple of accidents happened to me. I made mistakes, and I have learned tremendously from them. My main purpose is to inspire you to get up and get active—if you're not already doing so. Do not allow fear to let you think you're eliminating risk. If you're not game for climbing mountains, no problem. Get out there and become the best day hiker you can become to stay active and live a better life for you and your family. It doesn't take much. Know the level of risk you're willing to accept, and live with it. I have a good friend who knows his level of risk-taking because of a hiking experience that put him in a situation he wasn't comfortable with. Did he stop hiking? No! He's become an avid day hiker who enjoys the outdoors and regularly hikes with his wife to spend time together. By being active, you might just add another five quality years to your life!

In Lisa Harris' book *Building Your Enduring Fitness*, she states, "It's not that you can't walk anymore because you've gotten old; you've gotten old because you've stopped walking! Unfortunately, you start saying you can't or make excuses why you shouldn't get outside and just walk."

Ben Aldis, one of the Peloton instructors I work out to regularly, frequently quotes NFL player Jerry Rice, who famously said, "Today, I will do what others won't so that tomorrow I'll be able to do what others can't." That's a good motto to live by when you're young, but also when you get into your fifties and sixties. My plan is to keep climbing as long as I can. When I can't climb anymore, I plan on continuing to experience the outdoors by being an avid hiker, even if I'm so fortunate to live to one hundred! That is living.

WHAT I LEARNED LIVING WITH FEAR VS. AVOIDING RISK

Life involves some degree of risk. Different people can live with different levels of risk. Accepting risk is one thing; doing things to lower the chances of pushing risk too far is another. Stay on guard so you don't make choices that put you in bad situations.

Fear is healthy and can keep you alive. However, don't let fear stop you from doing fun things—even the most basic ways of being active.

FIVE THOUGHTS ON LIVING WITH FEAR VS. AVOIDING RISK

1. Be on guard while doing activities!
2. Sometimes it's not the first decision, but the careless ones that get you in trouble.
3. Remain or become active.
4. Know your risk level, live with it, and become active knowing it.
5. Risk can be good; fear keeps it safe.

SUMMARY

"Avoiding danger is no safer in the long run than outright exposure. The fearful are caught as often as the bold."

— Helen Keller

Some would consider climbing mountains to be risky. My desire to climb the Grand Teton might seem risky to people, but it ended up in a near-fatal end partially because of decisions we made, not exclusively because of the risk. Others wonder if people who climb and do other activities they're not familiar with have no fear. I believe we all have a certain amount of fear. People who do dramatically risky things have a degree of fear…that's how they're able to survive. Risk and fear live in the same universe.

Fear shouldn't keep you from being active though. *Staying* on guard does not just apply to people climbing mountains so they make the proper decisions before things go wrong. It can also be applied to people who are starting to become sedentary. They should be on guard that they are headed down a road where their life choices may quickly become limited because of inactivity.

So, I challenge you to live within your comfort level of risk, but still get out there and stay active for the sake of your family and your children. I challenge you to try new things and experience new activities that keep your legs moving so you're less limited as you age. Doing so will uplift both your physical energy and mental perspective on life. What do you have to lose?

CHAPTER 18

ENJOYING LIFE'S JOURNEY

"The two most important days in your life are the day
you're born and the day you find out why."

— Author Unknown

Over time, I've become respectful of people's beliefs. They believe what is true to them based on heritage, life lessons, learning, and exposure. For me, the event on June 30, 2022, was a life-altering experience. There is now the time before the accident and the time after. Life has made a shift for me. While I can't speak for Jim, I know we both feel God was there with us as we both struggled to save a life.

Many emotions have incubated over the past two years since that day. My immediate reaction was to think about the quote above that I had put on my computer screen soon after losing my job due to the global chaos that came with the spring of 2020. Little did I know then how relevant that quote would become.

When I returned home after the accident in the Tetons, I wrote some notes down, off and on while celebrating the Fourth of July weekend with my son and friends. I wrote as much as I could remember about what had happened and my thoughts at that time. I thought it was important to jot everything down while it was fresh, both from a therapeutic standpoint and so I would have an accurate remembrance of the day and the events. The advantage I had at that time was that I was in a soft cast from my ankle to mid-thigh, was still suffering from the pain of an enormous bruise, and regularly flashing back to being stuck underground next to that raging waterfall. I even went to the point of crudely sketching what it looked like in the ice moat on the ledge—the waterfall, the walls in front of me, and on both sides. I also drew what I remember as the last picture I had in my mind before entering that unknown hole.

That's also when I started the process of wondering *why*. While I truly believe in the quote above, I'm not sure that your why may not be realized until you're close to the end of your life, or after you're gone. Has the accident changed my life? How could it not? Gratitude comes to mind first. I've always been a person who might have taken life a little bit for granted. While some might feel my outdoor adventures were pushing the edge in the grand scheme of things, they didn't. Serious outdoors adventurers like Jimmy Chin, Ed Viesturs, Eric Honnold, Tommy Caldwell, and Conrad Anker are the true adventurers. I respect them immensely because they take huge, calculated chances. My adventures, risky to people who haven't spent a lot of time in the outdoors, pale in comparison to those of such phenomenal athletes. Even so, the risks taken in the outdoors are exhilarating, and I never really thought one of them could end my life. My thought was always, *When my time is up, it's up—that's part of life.* Since that time, I have grown to make sure I take time to appreciate every day, knowing there's a real possibility of it ending quickly.

Being a person who has believed in God my whole life (while not always living the saintly life), I've concluded that I need to be grateful for every day of my life going forward. As a remembrance to be grateful and to be humbled by the greatness of the ultimate plan, I have added a few things to my regular morning routine of exercises, stretching, and meditation. In addition to reading the Bible to get a handle on what's in it, I have also started praying on my knees. The last thing I do now is jot down a few comments about how I'm feeling that morning and three things I'm grateful for. Sometimes it's people; sometimes it's my surroundings. This practice grounds me to the fact that I woke up, walked to where I do the routine, and am headed into another day of unknowns with a feeling that I'm blessed compared to many people out there, and that I can tackle the day—whatever comes at me. The routine gets the day off in a positive direction.

I wouldn't have begun starting the day that way if not for my fall into the ice moat. Now, during the day, life sets in and I veer off the gratitude and thankfulness path. But by doing this practice every day, when I end up in my place of a short fuse or feeling anxious, the start of the day pays off because a gentle whisper comes to mind so I can slap myself back into reality, remember that things can go sideways at any time, and keep it all in perspective. Before the accident, while I was blessed in many ways, I tended not to appreciate all that was around me. Since the accident, I have continually reminded myself how fortunate I am and to try to get better.

"The sun shines not on us but in us. The
rivers flow not past, but through us."

— John Muir

The *why* I sometimes struggle with includes thinking about my friend Pete Matheson and why I'm alive and he's not. He was in the wrong spot when he fell off that hill just off the trail on the way down from Cot's Peak. The area and conditions weren't as severe as my fall into the ice moat, yet I'm here and he's not. We had hiked that trail at least a thousand times over the years while training to prepare for an adventure or just to get some exercise and enjoy the outdoors. He was in the wrong place at the wrong time. I fell into the deep ice moat because of negligence and carelessness. Some refer to this as survivor guilt, and I've tried to get my head around what causes the "Why?" guilt. While I'll never understand the reason, I know Pete would be pissed off to know I was beating myself up, and he would tell me to, "Stop your boohooing." Once again, I'm not sure of the master plan, but I try to take comfort in believing it's all for a reason, as much as it hurts.

The accident also causes me not to take the outdoors for granted. Over a fourteen-year period, I've been able to experience things many never do. Coming over the crest of the ridge at Cathedral Rocks high on Mount Rainer and seeing Little Tahoma and the expansive crevasses before me, forcing me to quickly stop because the view has taken my breath away, is a feeling I never get over. Some might think of my accident on the Grand Teton as a bad thing, but I'm eternally grateful. It's opened my eyes to so many things, and it has made me appreciate all the blessings we experience every day.

While I started climbing and being outdoors to get in better physical condition, it's become so much more. Being outdoors does so many things for so many people. For me, it's been a way to put life in perspective, and it has set me on a trajectory I never could have imagined. Whenever I'm down or need to reboot, the outdoors picks me up emotionally, helps me clear my head, and makes me realize how small we are in the grand scheme of things. However, it's not just the physical "being outdoors" that has benefited me. I've been given the best friends a person could have—they are true "If you had one last call, whom would you call?" friends. While the Yakima climbing group only connects occasionally via text or Facebook, I know we're always connected. That wouldn't have happened if it wasn't for the outdoors.

I've also met so many unique people I never would have been exposed to if not for the outdoors. After I "retired" from work because of the chaos of the lockdowns in 2020, I worked for REI as an adventure guide for a short time. The outdoors led me to that part-time job taking people on hikes (who might not have gone hiking previously) and going on backpacking trips with people from all walks of life.

Most importantly, this white, corporate capitalist benefited enormously from being around the other guides—most of whom were half my age. Most of them had other occupations during the week and worked part-time for REI on the weekends. Their occupations ran the gambit of the professional spectrum from someone who had multiple master's degrees to my good friends Garrett (the only other Baby Boomer in the group), Julie, and Sarah, who all have positive energy and lift me up every time we speak. I also would have never connected with Beth and Ruth, two amazing people who do unsung work I never would have heard about if not for my fall. My life would not be as rich if we hadn't had crossed paths. I had never been an "outdoorsy" type growing up, falling out of Boy Scouts after a couple of camping trips. Finding the outdoors in my late years has been therapeutic, both physically and mentally. Is that the *why*?

While some might look at a near-death experience as something to give you shivers, I look at it as an eternal blessing and a wakeup call. If not for the accident, I never would have experienced the lifesaving measures the National Park service performs everyday—at a pay level that reinforces they do it for the love of the outdoors, not the money. I never would have known how routinely the healthcare professionals at the Jackson hospital take life-saving measures and take care of people by cleaning them up, nursing their wounds, and then sending them on their way so they can do the same for numerous people every day. I never would have experienced how easily life can change simply by not making a half-hearted decision and taking a couple of minutes to unpack an ice ax. I never would have known what true friendship is when Jim dug into the side of a steep hill, risking falling into an unknown hole, to do what he could to save my life.

While I probably would have experienced the kindness I witnessed on my way to the Salt Lake City airport, at the rental car agency and the airline desk, I never would have noticed it because I would not have been so vulnerable. All the people just did what was the kind thing to do at the time to help a fellow human. I also never would have had the chance to experience the outpouring of love and sincere "Glad you're still here" comments from people if I hadn't had the accident. While my dad and I had a great relationship, I never would have known exactly how much he loved me when he told me he probably wouldn't have been able to go on if I had died that day in June 2022. Finally, I never would have been such a believer that actual, God-sent miracles happen and that I should thank God every day for the gift of another day of life.

WHAT I LEARNED

So, I don't really know my *why* or have enough experience to realize it. I do know some more reasons for life and how to enjoy it better. All these things are a result of the fall, which is a huge leap from where I was during my career when life centered around who was buying the food I was selling. That goal was very focused on trying to sell more and make certain I hit my quota while not always seeing what was going on around me. While I try to understand people's *why* now, if our two thoughts don't align on this subject, that's okay.

It's ironic that Simon Sinek, the world-famous inspirational speaker, author of the popular business book *Start with the Why*, and regular TedTalk contributor, talks about starting with the *why* in business, which makes sense. However, the *why* in life seems to come further down the road when you can identify it based on self-reflection on why you exist and the influence you have had on humanity or simply your friends and family.

FIVE THOUGHTS ABOUT ENJOYING THE JOURNEY

1. You don't need to search for your why. Let it happen.
2. Buy a bird app and listen—it helps you notice something you might not have.
3. When you open your eyes in the morning, say, "Thank you, God!"
4. Taking chances, even if they turn out badly, might just help with your *why*.
5. Being vulnerable rewards you with lessons.

SUMMARY

"Courage is the resistance to fear, mastery of fear, not the absence of fear."

— Mark Twain

I used to pray daily for God to show me my *why* after the accident in the Tetons. As part of his grand plan, I now believe that *why* is something that happens because of you enjoying life, looking around, talking to people, and being vulnerable. Those things help you get the most out of life.

The part I'm working on now can be summed up in two quotes. The first is by Mark Nepo: "The key to knowing joy is being easily pleased." The other is by Louis L'Amour: "The trail is the thing, not the end of the trail. Travel too fast, and you miss all you are traveling for." While I'm far from finding my exact *why*, I think I'm closer than I was before June 30, 2022. I'm hopeful I'll get there. I pray every day that I will.

My best advice to you on your journey to finding your *why* is to always stay on guard, live in the present moment, be grateful for all of your life's blessings, believe in miracles, be aware of your surroundings, and be confident that your life's *why* will appear slowly over time.

A FINAL NOTE

SAFELY PURSUING
YOUR WHAT IFS

"Climb the mountain not to plant your flag, but to embrace the challenge, enjoy the air and behold the view. Climb it so you can see the world, not so the world can see you."

— David McCullough, Jr.

The first steps toward climbing a mountain can be achieved by simply heading out your front door and walking around the block a few times. We can all do it. From there, you decide how to gradually increase your goals to start hiking regularly or the higher goal of climbing one of the many tall peaks in the US or around the world. All it takes is a regular routine, desire, and commitment. People do it at all ages, from all backgrounds, and from all walks of life. The only thing stopping you is you!

In 2018, country music legend Toby Keith wrote a song titled "Don't Let the Old Man In." In it, he sings about pushing back on age by asking how old you would be if you didn't know when you were born. Five-time Academy Award and two-time Oscar Award Winner, Clint Eastwood, the ninety-four-year-old actor, refers to aging as the old man and states that he works hard "not to let the old man in." This book hopefully addresses that dilemma in all of us. We all battle the conversation within ourselves, asking "What if?" versus deciding "Not anymore." So, what actions will you take right now, today, to *not* let the old man in?

In this book, you've seen the power that making aggressive goals can have and the ability to achieve them by coming up with a plan and then executing against that plan by finding people to help you set benchmarks. By having a step-by-step plan and working it (even when you don't feel like it), the emotion you can achieve when you successfully hit your goal will be elation. This book has reviewed living with fear versus avoiding risks. It also showed how facing death because of one small technical error can have a miraculous outcome. It told the story of making friends for life because of an outdoor activity that feeds the body, mind, and spirit—a rare occurrence.

Now, I challenge you to write out your top-ten challenges, or your outdoor adventures before you reach your "not anymore" stage. Your top-ten list doesn't necessarily need to be mountain climbing trips. It can be other adventures like hiking the El Camino trail, an expedition to Antarctica, or a hike to the top of Machu Picchu. I promise your life will be better because of pursuing these goals! In the ten exercise lines below, take a few minutes to write down your top-ten outdoor adventures or even exotic vacations:

1. _____

2. _____

3. _____

4. _____

5. _____

6. _____

7. _____

8. _____

9. _____

10. _____

Before I close, I want to leave you with two philosophies I've adopted over a lifetime and the past few years because of my accident in the Tetons. First, I draw from the quote above by Louis L'Amour, "The trail is the thing, not the end of the trail. Travel too fast, and you miss all you are traveling for." Life is short, so be safe, know your boundaries, and take time to breathe it all in.

Then I would say, "Things happen for you, not to you." It's a quote that removes any negative perspective and puts a positive light on life's twists and turns. Think about that. *Life happens for you, not to you.*

Now that you've finished reading my book, I encourage you to reach out to me. Tell me what you liked and didn't like about this book and how it can be improved. I would be sincerely interested to know your ten challenges and how they enlightened your life.

Thank you for taking the time to read my story! It's a journey that has had many thrills and includes activities I plan to continue to be involved with until I'm laid to rest. I wish you much success in achieving your goals and thinking about your "What ifs?" instead of your "Not anymores."

I wish all the best to you on your journey, and I always challenge you to *stay on guard*. Your family will thank you!

Dan Wenker

ABOUT THE AUTHOR

DAN WENKER is an author, speaker, outdoor enthusiast, avid mountaineer, and former REI outdoor experiences guide.

For more than fifteen years, Dan has been an avid mountaineer. Dan has summitted Mount Rainier (twice), Mount Kilimanjaro, Mount Whitney, Mount Adams (four times), Mount Hood, and Mount St. Helens (three times, including one time skiing). He is an avid skier whose favorite ski resorts are Big Sky, Montana; White Pass, Washington; and Grand Targhee, Wyoming.

After growing up in Philadelphia, Dan graduated from The Pennsylvania State University in 1981 where he received his Bachelor of Science degree in Agri-Business Management. His life made a dramatic turn several years later when he moved to Yakima, Washington, for work purposes and was exposed to the world of mountaineering, outdoor adventure, and backcountry skiing.

When not in the mountains, Dan has enjoyed a career in the foodservice industry as a foodservice sales/marketing executive and sales consultant.

Dan has been married to his forgiving wife, Mary, for thirty-seven years and counting. He has two grown children, Daniel and Caroline, plus a daughter-in-law and son-in-law. He splits his time between his and Mary's home in Atlanta, Georgia, and Jackson Lake in Monticello, Georgia. He loves sharing his experiences with others.

For more information on Dan Wenker, visit www.StayingOnGuard.org.

FOR MORE OF DAN WENKER'S OUTDOOR EXPERIENCES

Dan Wenker is happy to be a guest speaker for your group or a podcast guest and share his outdoor experiences, his thoughts on planning an outdoor adventure, and what he did to pivot his life toward the outdoors. His experiences will help you discover how easily you can have adventures of your own.

For a complimentary consultation or pre-speaking interview, text or email him or visit his website. Please include your name, time zone, and the best time to call you.

www.StayingOnGuard.org

wnkrdan@gmail.com

(509) 654-2205